# GET FIT WITH BICYCLING

*by the editors of **Bicycling**® magazine*

Text by
David L. Smith, M.D.
Eugene A. Gaston, M.D.
of the *Bicycling*® staff

Printed in the United States of America on recycled paper, containing a high percentage of de-inked fiber.

Cover photograph by Sally Ann Shenk
Book series design by K. A. Schell

**Library of Congress Cataloging in Publication Data**

Smith, David Lynn, 1942-
    Get fit with bicycling.

    1. Cycling—Addresses, essays, lectures. 2. Physical fitness—Addresses, essays, lectures.    3. Cycling—Physiological aspects—Addresses, essays, lectures.
I. Gaston, Eugene A., joint author.    II. Bicycling!
III. Title.
GV1041.S57        796.6        79-16236
ISBN 0-87857-283-X                    paperback

          10    9              paperback

# Contents

## Contents

# Introduction

I feel reasonably sure that the next physical fitness boom in this country will center not only on activities that one can participate in for a lifetime, but on activities that are as much life-style as lifesport.

I think this development will be the result of a natural social evolution, a desire on the part of Americans to integrate all aspects of their lives more fully. That is, I suspect people, particularly those pressed by time and responsibilities, will be less interested in giving over a chunk of their lives to a particular exercise and will pursue activities that don't announce such a sharp division between their active and passive days. Certainly there's no fitter candidate to integrate the ragged ends of our hectic days than the bicycle.

All of us have met individuals who are intolerable if they haven't spent a certain amount of time exercising. I would guess that this attitude comes from the real or imagined belief that a person gets some kind of health guarantee if he or she invests a certain amount of time in strenuous exercise.

We know that new evidence is emerging that indicates a surprisingly small amount of exercise will benefit the heart. Researchers have found that a minimum of 30 minutes of vigorous physical activity per week is associated with "protection" against coronary artery disease (J. N. Morris, et al. "Vigorous Exercise in Leisure-Time and the Incidence of Coronary Heart-Disease." *Lancet.* 17 February 1973, pp. 333–39).

Commenting on a study involving 17,000 men, Ralph S. Paffenberger, M.D., Stanford University School of Medicine, told the American Heart Association that if people burn up 2,000 calories a week they can reduce the risk of a heart attack by 64 percent (*Washington Post*, 22 October 1978).

In the same article, author Richard M. Restak raises some interesting questions about individuals under stress taking up stressful exercises for relief. In other words, they exercise stressfully.

> What is exceedingly troubling is that many other converts to the exercise cult may be individuals already facing a high risk of coronary heart disease because of their psychological makeup.
>
> It is becoming generally recognized that, along with biological and environmental factors, a particularly aggressive, ambitious and competitive behavior pattern, commonly associated with what are known as "Type A" personalities, confers an additional coronary-disease risk of more than 30 percent. There is also evidence suggesting that precisely such persons are engaging in the strenuous exercise crusade with the same sense of urgency and competitiveness, the determination to run that extra mile or go that extra lap across the pool or prove some other point.

While it is clear that researchers need to explore the above points more fully, surely our chosen exercise shouldn't contribute to the stress already too abundant in our lives.

Is it a peculiarly American habit to view exercise along a one-dimensional, linear plane, an investment that should reap quick and guaranteed rewards? I don't know the answer to this. A British cyclist, Keith Matthews, seems to think such is the case, suggesting in a tongue-in-cheek letter that even cyclists fall victim to this thinking:

> U.S. cyclists, as portrayed by your journal, seem obsessed with health and cardiovascular conditioning. My experience of U.S. cyclists bears a lot of this out. By the time the helmet has been put on, the rear mirror adjusted, correct clothing put on and the limbering up completed, most normal riders will be 10 miles down the road.

Actually, there is some very good thinking in Britain these days on the subject of cycling as life-style. I refer to a remarkable collection of papers, *Cycling: The Healthy Alternative*, prepared for the British Cycling Bureau. (The 90-page report can be obtained from the British Cycling Bureau, Stanhope House, Stanhope Place, London W2 2HH England, price: $9.) Written by 10 experts in different areas of medicine, social studies, and planning, *Cycling* is marked by a diversity and richness of thinking. The book goes a long way toward defining the lifesport of cycling as a life-style.

Dr. David Kerr, a general practitioner in London, writes in his chapter, "Psychological Aspects of Cycling," that unlike other forms of transport which tend to alienate people from each other, cycling helps create bonds between individuals. With some humor, Dr. Kerr writes that:

> Modern forms of transport alienate the transported not only from the territory they traverse but also from the inhabitants they trespass upon. It is an evidently practical procedure for the hungry male to chat up the enticing female from within the confines of a sports car—indeed, the perpetuation of the race often seems to depend on his success. But the car needs to be stationary (or nearly so) for the courtship to have productive end. Wooing, as an active human practice, is more easily conducted from the saddle of a slow-moving bicycle, ensuring a more pro-longed and more visual confrontation with the subject.
>
> Less flippantly, this ready relationship with other pedestrians (as well as other cyclists, and even motorists held immobile for long periods on urban roads), provides one more humanizing dimension for the act of cycling, in marked contrast to the isolation which so bleakly charac-terizes other forms of transport.

Commenting on the psychotherapeutic role of cycling, Dr. Kerr writes that:

> Cycling, like other activities which promote body func-tions outside and beyond the daily norm, inevitably brings with it a revised perspective of our body shape and the way it works. As the practice of exercise increases, function improves. As function improves, so awareness of function grows, promoting confidence in the ability to control and direct it. Steadily, the active exerciser sheds the fears and misapprehensions about the way his body works which underpin much psychosomatic illness.

Picking up on this theme another contributor, Mayer Hillman, Ph.D., states that:

> Exercise entailed in cycling can be said to have a tran-quilizing effect with the result that we are far less likely to

arrive at our destination fretful after a tedious or stressful journey by bus or car—perhaps medical science one day will be able to establish cycling as a suitable means for dissipating aggression.

Perhaps the bicycle's most attractive social virtue is that cycling can raise the mobility of the majority of the population—who do not have the optional use of a car. Its potential near-universal availability can enable people of all ages, provided they are reasonably fit, to travel at 10 or 15 mph. (Elderly cyclists attest to the fact that aging is by no means a deterrent and for people with some arthritic conditions, it may be easier to cycle than to walk.) However, cycling does not reduce other people's mobility; this is in marked contrast to the car, for there is increasing evidence of the fact that the more who travel by car, the less mobile everyone else becomes.

We know that cycling can keep the heart and muscles strong for a lifetime and do so gently and rhythmically, without stress. That is a desirable lifesport.

But, as the authors of *Cycling: The Healthy Alternative* suggest, the bicycle is not merely an exercise tool. It certainly serves that function and serves it well. Yet indications are that cycling can make positive contributions to the way we live, to our life-style. The bicycle is a way to humanize ourselves and the space around us. When you invest in a bike you invest in people.

And the following examples suggest how cycling can take you to fitness and beyond.

James C. McCullagh
Editor
*Bicycling* magazine

## Case One: Uncle Loyd

Susan Weaver

That my great-uncle Loyd has lived to 107 and that much of his adult life he bicycled to work in rural Missouri (until the bicycle retired before he did), I never connected. I just look on it as another facet of the intriguing life of this spry, raspy-voiced little man, who began book learning in a one-room schoolhouse and moved by covered wagon with his family at age eight from Bewleyville,

Kentucky, to Jasper, Missouri. Perhaps because he was a twin, he was always small. Soon after he and his brother were born, his grandfather, a tall, door-filler of a man, pronounced them poor specimens of humanity. "Louisa will never raise those babies," he prophesied, "and if she does, they won't have any sense."

"He missed it on the first part, and the second part of it, I don't know," Loyd once observed with a dry wit that fairly crackles sometimes.

Despite the prediction, he was sturdy. An active farm boy who, at age 7, walked 21 miles to school and 21 miles home again, he grew into a man who bought his first bicycle before most of us were even around to think about it. That was 1898; he was in his late twenties. A few years later he bought an old bicycle frame that needed rejuvenating, and, as he tells it, "sometimes in the East they used to sell a collection to work over old bicycles. Well, I sent and got me one of these; it had two wheels, handlebars, and tires—double tires in those days—and I used it to fix up that bike. I rode to and from my job in a store for 17 years. I just wore it out." At this point he was 50, and his wife and daughter scuttled his idea of buying a new one; "too many automobiles they said," and that was 1921.

Still, that sense of independence common to cyclists was unsinkable, and he walked to work, then home for the noon meal, then back to work, and home again, walking four or five miles a day until he retired.

What does it mean? Cycling, walking, and gardening, too, were his life-style. He grew his own fresh vegetables for years, and even on the day of his 100th birthday party he spent a few hours in the backyard, nurturing tender green things. In fact, as a birthday present, someone arranged to have a seed company name a new variety of sweet corn after him. Hardaway's Gold it was called.

If we continue to cycle, will we live to be 100? Who knows, but Loyd Hardaway can't blame it on his genes. His twin brother Luther, "a fat fellow . . . not excessively fat, but he outweighed me 40 pounds," had diabetes and died of a heart attack at 59.

Nor does the number of our years matter quite so much as enhancing the quality of those we do have, although the two often go hand in hand.

## Case Two: Up-and-Coming Starr

Klasina VanderWerf

Oliver Starr is a Midget class bicycle racer from Denver, Colorado, whose age, at 10, sometimes puts him literally in a class by

5

himself. A member of the Rocky Mountain Road Club, he races against riders in the Intermediate class (13 to 15 years) who are not only older, but who are also allowed to have higher gears on their bikes. "In one race," relates Oliver, "I got dropped because on the backstretch there was a huge tailwind and a downhill. I just couldn't crank fast enough to keep up."

But Oliver doesn't let that stop him, since racing is the focus of his youthful energies and a catalyst for growth that even he may be unaware of. His spirit is not easily daunted, and he seeks out the good ride. When it was time to qualify for a berth in the National races in Milwaukee, Wisconsin, there was Starr, raring to go. "I was the only one, so all I had to do was show up. But I rode anyway."

This steady persistence is the way Oliver earned his Flying Dutchman bicycle. First he earned a biking jersey from his parents by riding a distance of 25 miles in less than 3 hours. For the bike, Oliver's father, Ken, set up a 13½-mile course that Oliver had to complete in under 50 minutes. "I had to practice, but I did it in 48 minutes."

"I got the idea of racing into my head by myself. I just said, 'Dad, I'm going to race.' He didn't take me seriously. It made me mad. So, after the first race, I decided to do better."

Doing better has become a habit, Oliver placed 13th in the Midget class in this year's Nationals, but his goal for next year is "to place in the top three."

Oliver goes about achieving his goals methodically. He has already devoured "all the books on bicycles we have in the house" and has mapped out strategies for himself based on his reading.

His training is carefully thought out. He begins the season by riding long distances, starting at about 30 miles a day. Then, as the Nationals draw near, he shortens his daily rides to about 12 miles, concentrating on hard-time trials.

Because of a bout with pneumonia, Oliver had to stop training for a month in the spring. "It took two days of riding to get my lungs back in shape," he says. "I felt I had better form after the layoff. I think I was overtraining."

Oliver tries to do most of his own maintenance. He learned the importance of that the hard way when, during a race, his chainring started to come off because the bolts hadn't been tightened properly. "I lost the race. I didn't even finish," he'll comment quietly. "I don't think it's so important as to how you take a bike apart as how you put it back together."

Toward food, Oliver's attitude is more responsible even than most adults. During training he avoids ice cream, candy, and soda. "My willpower died a bit once, and I had some ice cream," he admits. Then Oliver will make a doughnut around one wrist with his other hand and say, "I'm the skinniest kid in my class. Runners and cyclists have the lowest percentage of body fat of anybody."

Obviously there is no correlation between size and success. Though he races against older riders, Oliver has had some impressive wins. He placed third overall in the Intermediate class in the Denver Tech Center Criterium and third in the Mount Evans Hill Climb along the highest auto route in the nation.

Oliver's sights are set high. "I wanna be good," he emphasizes, eyeing his bike. "I may be good in my category, but I'm not good compared to the top riders in the state." He hesitates. "But I've got time."

## Case Three: Racing Sheriff

Alice Nass

Just about every day at lunch a 52-year-old sheriff in the Los Angeles area rides his bicycle. He rides for pleasure, he rides to train, and he rides to save his heart. "It's amazing to me," Rudy Berteaux marvels. "About 15 years ago they discovered I had high blood pressure and problems with my heart cardiogram—it showed irregularities. (In fact, I'd had a heart attack but we didn't realize it.) I weighed 200 and some pounds. I had lots of trouble breathing; I could barely mow the lawn; so they told me to exercise."

During the next five years he began jogging, improved his eating habits, and reduced to 185. Because his knees eventually hurt him, he had to give up running, but fortunately he had begun cycling for pleasure. He started enjoying the scenery and riding with a bike club. So he stepped up the cycling and began competing four years ago.

The man who formerly had to stay in bed just to keep his blood pressure down was soon winning medals. In the California Police Olympics two years ago he took two silver medals in the over-40 category. Last year, just to see how he'd fare, he entered open competition and won a gold in the sprints, "which was a super surprise." He also copped two silver medals in the 10-mile criterium and the 30-mile road race. "So I've been getting better."

That is an understatement indeed. With the California team he entered the International Police Olympics, "and we had guys from all over the country and from Europe. I got a third place in the open in the 25-mile. The guys who beat me were 25 . . ." He's twice their age.

His training is regular and monitored by his doctor with twice-yearly stress tests. "He keeps telling me, 'Go at it! It's the best thing you can do,' " Rudy smiles. Averaging about 150 miles a week, he rides back and forth to work 20 miles each way in summer. In winter he gets up early and bikes 10 or 15 miles on good mornings and an hour at lunchtime.

He is enthusiastic about the change in himself. "I look good, I feel trim. And it's nice to have a cardiologist tell you, 'You're in great shape. Go out there and ride that 30-miler.' I just can't get over the fact that people don't realize what they can do if they want to. If they get out there every day and jog, they'll get better; if they get out there on that bike, they can ride to work. . . ."

It's exciting to know Rudy and what he's done. It's equally pleasing to know that he is not alone. He tells us, in fact, about the Ranch Los Amigos Hospital cycling club, comprised entirely of riders who bike for rehabilitation as well as sport. Organized in 1974 by Randy Ice, a therapist at the hospital, the club accepts cyclists only after their coronary disease shows some degree of stability. Most have participated in a training program conducted at the hospital; there they have been monitored while exercising on a bicycle ergometer or treadmill, and they monitor themselves at home. They get started on a proper diet and give up cigarettes if they smoke. Eventually they phase into the Saturday club.

"The camaraderie in the group is just unbelievable," reports Ice. "The big thing for most patients when they have heart diseases is that they are very depressed and uncertain about what they can and cannot do. When they get into a group of people like this who are making incredible improvements—some rapidly and some slowly, but improving—it gives them the chance to talk to other guys about their problem."

At 73, one member recently completed his third century, Randy tells us. "We rode from Fullerton to San Diego in one day; he found it was easy for him. He'd had a cancer operation in 1951 and about 2½ years ago had an aortic aneurysm as well as bypass surgery. He'd never cycled before. When he came to me, he was 69 years old and wasn't really doing anything. Now he's so interested in cycling, he knows more about the technical aspects of bicycles and components than I do. He rides about 500 to 600 miles a month."

It isn't easy to get started, but the supervision helps. Knowing how to pace yourself and how far to ride in the beginning are important. One plus-50 cyclist who began without such guidance describes how difficult it was for her at first. "I am a 'bikey' now," writes the woman, whose cycling is therapy for a cardiomyopathy, "a charley horse of the heart muscle," as she calls it.

Three years ago I just went in and bought a 10-speed, and with no technical knowledge, purchased what I thought was suitable. I then attempted to participate in various club rides. This I did, always unsure as to the difficulty of the ride and my capabilities. I suffered them out, many times finding myself alone, trying to read the map. Sometimes I would cry right in the middle of a ride, wondering what I was doing to myself. Eventually I would find my way back, coming home tired and feeling so good about myself I knew I wanted to try again."

One afternoon on a ride she met a man who looked like Colonel Sanders on a bicycle. "He led rides independently and actually taught me how to use those gears; slow and easy. He had not taken up bicycling until his sixties and had experienced a previous heart attack. His rides were geared to his riders, the terrain, traffic, and wind factor, if possible. This experience started me on my way, and I was now convinced I could be a bikey.

"Since that time I rode with another man, a loving friend who was a cyclist all his life. I was introduced to rides and outings on which mature bikeys take the time to look around and enjoy. We experienced bicycle rides that made a one-day outing seem like a whole vacation.

"Today, 2½ years later, my health problem seems to be gone, I no longer take any medication, and it is like I have a whole new body."

Even the death of her cycling friend has not changed her mind. "It was just a few months ago, while experiencing a beautiful ride through a remote canyon that my loving friend, just ahead of me, leaned over on his bicycle. His time had run out; God had His way to take him. My friend loved cycling so much, it was his way too.

"Life goes on, and bicycling still is the answer. Women and men both need to stay active. We need the outings and camping experiences geared to our abilities; life becomes rich and full for us again."

## Case Four: Out of Retirement

Victor L. Hadlock

One day in March 1977, word was passed down that the boss wanted to see me at the end of my shift. Less than a week earlier, I had handed in my notice. At the age of 65, I was retiring from my job as a security officer for Atlanta's largest hotel.

I couldn't take being on my feet constantly for eight hours a night. I had an arthritic back, collapsed metatarsals, and constant pain in my legs. Besides, I no longer wanted to risk being bounced to the sidewalk in front of the hotel by a mean drunk.

Randy was in his office when I entered. He went right to the point. "Vic," he said, "you still have a little over a week to go on your notice if you want to, but I know you're in constant pain, so why not take off now? You won't lose any pay."

I took him up on it, and the first few weeks were great. I fished; I read; I loafed.

But I soon tired of those things. Besides, my back and legs still hurt; I felt as though I were walking with shoes full of gravel. Climbing the stairs to the second floor was a major operation. Trips to the doctor had produced a maximum of pills and a minimum of relief.

Somewhere, I had read that exercise, with good judgment and a doctor's approval, was beneficial in some arthritis cases, and good for high blood pressure, which I had, too.

Things seem to come to me late in life. At 58, not having bicycled for 25 years, I got the bug again. On a shopping trip through a discount store, I paused by the bicycle display. Somebody warned me I would have a heart attack "at my age," but I bought one anyway—a Columbia 3-speed.

After a few months of playing around with my bike, I had put it in the basement and all but forgotten it. Now at 65, I thought of it again. I got it out, cleaned and oiled it, and started my program. I purchased the paperback, *Cycling: The Rhythmic, Respiratory Way to Physical Fitness* (New York: Grosset & Dunlap, 1968).

My roadwork was off to a shaky start with a couple of pedal-turns and a prompt spill in my own driveway. I dumped a few more times before I got the feel of it again. But fortunately, I am a small man, and I learned a long time ago how to fall. No bones were broken and only my dignity was bruised.

I soon decided, however, that if I were to get anywhere with my idea, I needed a bike in better shape, at least, than I was. So, it was off to the bike store.

There was a confusing array of models, mostly 10-speeds. Somehow I couldn't see myself crouched hunchback over a set of upside-down handlebars, working complicated gears with shifters on a hard-to-reach down tube. Suddenly, I saw my bike; a black beauty, sleek and well engineered. The decal said: Raleigh LTD III, and it bore the proud legend "Made in England" on the top tube.

Go ahead and laugh, you young jocks, who think the only thing worth riding is a 10- or 12-speed with exotic pedigree. I can take anything after the patronizing smile of the bike shop owner.

So the 3-speed is too slow? Well, the doctor told me not to try to win any races. It's too heavy? Anyone who can't manage a well-made 3-speed around town, to the store, to visit friends, or on a five- or six-mile exercise ride ought to put a down payment on a luxury-model rocking chair, or so I said.

The first month was murder. I was not only out of condition, I was 65. I had painful arthritis in the lumbar region of my back. My left leg continually felt as though I had just pulled it out of a fire, not to mention my aching feet.

Ten or fifteen minutes was the longest ride I could manage for the first few weeks. The slightest upgrade was a huffing, puffing, heart-pounding challenge. When a ride was over, I could hardly make it from the garage to the back door. I would collapse on the living room couch and rest for half an hour.

The second month was somewhat better. The little hills around my home were still giving me trouble, but I was conquering them in low gear. My leg muscles, slowly accustoming themselves to the daily routine, were getting stronger and hurting less.

By the end of the third month, I was staying out about an hour and beginning to enjoy it. Those hills, which had seemed like mountains at first, were giving me no trouble now, even in second gear. I was no longer gasping for breath and was able to ride the white line at the right side of the road without wobbling all over the place.

It's over a year now since I purchased my racer, which of course, it isn't. I no longer get the car out to go a short mile for a newspaper or to go to the bank; I use the bike. I am a familiar sight to mail carriers, police, and shopkeepers in my town. An old man on a bike gets a lot of smiles, even from pretty girls.

I'd like to say that after a year, all of my aches and pains are gone. But I'm a truthful man. I still have occasional pain in my lower back, and my left leg gives me a little trouble now and then. All of this, however, is less severe and less frequent. My blood pressure is under control. My general health is excellent, not to mention my increased stamina and improved mental and emotional outlook.

I'd like to caution old codgers who, like me, may be considering bicycling to restore youthful vigor. Don't go off the deep end. Before you even straddle the saddle, have a good physical. Make sure all your vital signs are in order. Then, if the doctor deems it advisable, make haste slowly.

Don't overdo it. You could do more harm than good. If the hills are too great a challenge, dismount and walk. Don't strain your lungs until you're gasping for breath. (I did, but I shouldn't have.) For the first few months, rest after each ride to let your body catch up. Act your age now, so you can act younger later.

As I look back, I'm glad I didn't yield to that little demon-voice that kept whispering, "You're too old for this foolishness; quit while you're ahead!" I shall be ever grateful to that doctor who said: "You ought to ride it every day." In return when I look at his ample paunch, I am tempted to say: "Why don't you try it, Doc?" But I keep my mouth shut.

11

# Part One
# The Lifesport

# Getting Started

## John Schubert and Kathy Keck

*1. What type of bicycle should I buy?*

Different types of bicycles are best suited for different uses. For riding around town or short commutes, the 3-speed bike, which requires little maintenance, is the most practical. But for recreational riding, hilly terrain, or long distances, the mechanical and biological advantages of the 10-speed make it the best choice. A 10-speed is far better if you seek to use your bicycle for exercise.

*2. How can I tell whether a bike fits me?*

While wearing flat-soled shoes, straddle the top tube of a men's bicycle frame. There should be about an inch clearance between your crotch and the top tube. (If you wish to purchase a women's frame, first make this test on a men's frame and then find a women's frame on which the seat tube is the same length as the proper-size men's frame.) You'll find a too-small frame uncomfortable to ride; a too-large frame is both uncomfortable and dangerous. You'll probably want to extend the seatpost a few inches when you have a frame that's right for you. And since not everyone has the same-size arms, you may need a longer or shorter handlebar stem than the one that comes with the bicycle.

*3. What type of handlebars should my bicycle have?*

For the most beneficial exercise, for long rides, and for hill climbing, you'll want to have the dropped (racing style) handlebars seen on 10-speed bicycles. Dropped bars look uncomfortable, and they are for your first few rides, but most cyclists grow to prefer them. They rearrange your body to provide many biomechanical advantages. But if your back can't get used to dropped bars or if you don't anticipate long rides, you may want to join the many people who stick with upright handlebars.

### 4. *What type of saddle should my bicycle have?*

This depends on your handlebars. A wide saddle works well with upright handlebars. If you have dropped handlebars, you'll find the wide saddle uncomfortable. Racing-style saddles, like racing-style handlebars, are quite functional and more comfortable than they look. Women, who have wider pelvic bones than men, generally need a slightly wider version of the racing-style saddle.

### 5. *How fast should I pedal?*

Many new cyclists make the mistake of selecting a high gear and try to exercise themselves by pushing at it as hard as they can. Although this makes you feel tired, it isn't very good exercise, and it's not the easiest or fastest way to ride. Select a gear low enough so that you can barely feel any effort to spin the pedals. Spin the pedals at a smooth clip, with the pedal revolutions per minute (usually called cadence) a bit quicker than your pulse—maybe 70 revolutions per minute. If this cadence makes you feel uncomfortable, slow down and work up to this level gradually. Remember that pedaling should always feel smooth, free, and easy.

### 6. *How long and how far should I ride?*

When first starting to bicycle, ride for about 15 or 20 minutes; then get off your bike and rest. See how long it takes your heartbeat and breathing to return to normal. When you feel comfortable riding for this length of time, increase your distance and vary the terrain.

### 7. *Should I use toe clips?*

You'll probably want to start out without toe clips and get used to your bicycle without them. But once you're used to your bicycle, you'll want toe clips. They increase your pedaling efficiency by holding your feet in the optimum position on the pedals. With toe clips, pedaling becomes a smooth 360-degree motion instead of a jerking push–push. Toe clips help you get more exercise out of your bicycle, and they help you enjoy an afternoon ride without getting tired.

### 8. *How should I use the gears?*

Whether your bicycle has 3 speeds, 10, or even more, the purpose of the gears is to allow you to maintain constant cadence and pedaling effort in spite of varying terrain and wind conditions.

The many gears on a 10-speed allow you to pick the ideal gear for prevailing conditions, whereas a 3-speed offers you a more limited selection. Learning to deftly shift a 10-speed means thinking ahead. It takes time and practice.

### 9. *How does bicycling benefit me physically?*

Regular exercise on a bicycle makes your heart more oxygen enriched, powerful, and efficient. Cycling improves circulation, muscle tone, digestion, and weight control. It is a complete form of exercise—beneficial to your legs, arms, shoulders, back, diaphragm, and abdominal muscles.

### 10. *When out for a day's ride, what should I eat?*

Eat light and give yourself plenty of digesting time before starting out again when you stop for meals. You might want to carry some fresh fruit or dried fruits and nuts to munch on as you are riding. Also, carry plenty of liquids (fruit juice or water) and drink frequently along the way.

### 11. *What would be a good bicycle fitness/training program to follow?*

The American College of Sports Medicine makes the following recommendations for training to develop and maintain fitness:

a) Frequency of training—three to five days per week;
b) Intensity of training—60 to 90 percent of your maximum heart-rate reserve (220 minus age in years minus resting pulse rate);
c) Duration of training—15 to 60 minutes of continuous aerobic exercise.

### 12. *Can I use the bicycle to lose weight?*

Frequent exercise expends a significant number of calories and can help in weight control. But diet must also be taken into consideration for weight loss. Get at least 20 minutes of vigorous exercise every day. Start with a 1,000- to 1,200-calorie-a-day diet if you desire to lose weight and try not to ingest more than 2,500 calories a day at the maximum. Most importantly, keep your fat intake low.

### 13. *How many hours do I need to ride each week to get maximum physical benefit from cycling?*

You should try to ride for at least 20 to 30 minutes a day which would total about 3½ hours a week. By doing this you will maintain cardiovascular tone and prevent loss of muscle tissue.

**14. Why is cycling to be recommended over other fitness activities, such as jogging?**

Because of the smoothness involved in riding, the legs don't pound a surface as they do in jogging; therefore, there is less chance of tearing injuries to muscles or connective tissue. You can spend more time cycling than you perhaps could in other activities, and you can continue it for a lifetime.

**15. Can I get enough exercise cycling back and forth to school, work, and the store?**

Amounts of exercise derived from commuting for any purpose depend on such factors as distance, level of terrain, and your cadence. The degree of enough exercise varies from person to person. Regular usage of a bicycle for short trips will condition your muscles and your cardiovascular system and is thereby an important means of providing exercise. If you don't feel as if you are receiving enough exercise from your commutes, it may be beneficial for you to do some short-distance touring on weekends if time allows.

**16. How do I maintain my level of fitness during winter and inclement weather?**

When you can't ride due to weather conditions, you can use indoor stationary-cycle exercise machines or rollers. Rope-skipping is also helpful for all-over toning.

**17. Are there warm-up exercises I should be doing before I cycle?**

Because cycling tends to tighten the hamstring muscles in the backs of the thighs, it is a good idea to warm up before riding. You can keep these muscles stretched and limber by doing toe touches and lower leg stretches—stand three feet in front of a wall with your feet two inches apart. Place outstretched hands on the wall, keeping your feet flat on the floor. Move your feet away from the wall, keeping them flat on the floor through the whole exercise.

**18. Where can I go to get a basic understanding about using my bike efficiently?**

Talk to your local bike shop owner. He or she would be happy to familiarize you with the mechanics of a bicycle and perhaps help you to choose a bike that you would like to buy. Also, join a local cycling club. Experienced members can help provide you with hints on commuting and touring in your local area.

*19. What are the health risks of riding a bike in polluted air?*

Recent studies have shown that a cyclist is less vulnerable to environmental pollutants than car drivers. However, experienced cyclists tend to seek out less-polluted roadways for cycling.

*20. What are the advantages of using cycling as an exercise tool?*

Cycling is convenient. You can get your exercise while you commute or run errands. The exercise does not jar the joints because it is gentle and rhythmic. Cycling is an exercise that you can participate in all of your life.

*21. How many calories do you expend cycling for one hour?*

The average expenditure of calories for moderate bike riding is estimated to be 300 calories per hour. Here is formula that you can use to calculate how many calories you burn in one hour of cycling: $C = 0.8(0.053 \text{ VW} + 0.083 \text{ V}^3)$ where C = calories per hour; V = velocity in miles per hour; and W = weight of the cyclist plus bicycle.

*22. What exercises complement cycling?*

Cross-country skiing and speed skating are the two exercises which come closest to cycling in use of muscles and overall conditioning. However, running, rope-skipping, and hiking can also be beneficial to your cycling abilities.

*23. Do you get psychological benefits from cycling?*

Cyclists who ride for fitness frequently claim as much psychological as physical benefit from the sport. *Cycling: The Healthy Alternative,* which is referred to in the Introduction, suggests some of the psychological benefits of cycling.

Dr. John H. Greist who has used running to treat moderate depression feels that "Bicycling, cross-country skiing, walking, rowing, canoeing, swimming—any program that uses large muscle masses in regular rhythm—should have the same effect."

*24. Is a medical examination necessary before I begin cycling?*

It is recommended that everyone first have a thorough physical examination by their doctor before starting any type of exercise program. Even if you are young, your cardiovascular system could possibly be out of shape if it is not accustomed to strenuous exercise.

Also, people over 40 years old who have not had a long-term commitment to physical fitness may have an increased risk of heart attack or muscle damage. These people should not engage in strenuous exercise without a thorough medical evaluation and physical-fitness training. Most important, once you have your doctor's approval, start out slowly in your exercise program. Your body needs time to acclimate itself to this new activity.

# Part Two
# Exercise and Nutrition

# The Cyclist's Body Type

### David L. Smith, M.D.

A long-distance runner is a collection of bones, as the spiritual tells us, which are connected together by a few tendons and ligaments and covered with a thin skin. The whole thing is designed to flop and flap down the road with a minimum of energy expended. A body-builder, in contrast, appears designed for maximum energy expenditure. He or she is a collection of striated muscle, with whatever amounts of bone and connective tissue that are necessary to accomplish tasks usually reserved for bulldozers and cranes. The difference between the two, expressed in scientific terms, is somatotyping.

A person's somatotype depends on the relative abundance of fat and muscle. Fatness is endomorphy; heavy bone and muscle development is called mesomorphy; and a relative lack of either is called ectomorphy. Each of these three components is graded on a scale of 1 to 9. Thus an extreme endomorph would be a 911; extreme mesomorph a 191; and extreme ectomorph, 119. These numbers can be estimated by eyeballing or by a complicated series of measurements. Endomorphy is defined by the sum of several skinfold measurements. Mesomorphy is measured by a series of measurements of bone diameter and arm and leg circumferences, corrected for skinfold thickness and for height. Ectomorphy can be calculated from the height divided by the cube root of the weight.

Within limits, of course, the somatotype depends on diet and exercise. Lots of food and no exercise leads to an increase in endomorphy, whereas lack of food will lead to ectomorphy. Mesomorphy depends on exercise, but there is probably a bigger hereditary component for mesomorphy than for the other two characteristics.

What somatotype should the cyclist be? I suppose that the ideal cyclist would be a rather peculiar-looking animal—a 191 from the waist down and maybe a 154 from the waist up (a certain amount of development of the arms being necessary to control the handlebars and brakes). Fat is of no use at all, but the cyclist could probably get away with more fat than a distance runner would.

Actually, a study of Olympic athletes in 1974 showed that the average male Olympic cyclist was about a 253. Their build was very close to that of sprinters and swimmers. Basketball players and distance runners were only slightly less muscular than cyclists, near 254, rather than being extreme ectomorphs. Most other athletes, including boxers, rowers, and divers, were slightly more muscular than cyclists, with somatotypes near 252, 263, and 363. Weight lifters were 271s, while the average male spectator was closest to 342 and the average female spectator, 542. Spectators, I suppose, need lots of insulation and padding for sitting on hard benches at cold football games.

What does all this mean? I guess it means that to be a good racing or touring cyclist, you don't have to depend on luck, to be either very tall or very muscular. All you need is a sensible diet and Eddy Merckx's secret: "Ride lots!"

# Aerobic Training

## David L. Smith, M.D.

The human body is a bigger source of wind resistance than all the protruding bolts, water bottles, flags, and bags that could be installed on a bike. To this end, racers and wise tourists try to minimize their wind resistance by crouching over the handlebars as far as possible. I have even seen a dandy young fellow whose rear end was higher than his head and shoulders. To the end of getting down on the drops, putting the seat as far forward as possible will usually make this much easier. Losing some fat around the middle helps flexibility (and weight) a lot.

Most Americans, and many bicyclists including myself, weigh too much. It's much cheaper (but not easier) to take 10 pounds off your skeleton than off your bicycle. Probably more than 15 percent body fat for men, or 25 percent for women, is too much. Except for Eskimos, who needs the insulation? Who is more than 15 percent fat? Look at a picture of the front-runners at a marathon race. Then look in a full-length mirror.

Here's a rule of thumb for determining body fat. For a man, pinch the skin on the back, just below the tip of the right shoulder blade. The skinfold (which should be oriented up and down) will probably not be thicker than 15 millimeters. For women, there is a complicated formula relating to skinfolds on the back of the arm and the side of the abdomen. Fifteen percent or less body fat is very difficult for a woman to achieve, due to less muscle mass. For women, 20 to 25 percent is more realistic.

To get miles and miles out of the legs every day, day in and day out on a long tour, there's no substitute for conditioning. You are just going to have to get out there and ride more miles every day and every week until your legs will deliver whatever distance you want. With sufficient conditioning, even middle-aged nonathletes can ride 100 or more miles a day. Short rides around town, no matter how hard you ride, just won't produce the endurance capacity necessary.

The final common source of energy for the motion of muscles is a molecule called ATP. There are three chemical pathways for the production of ATP: from glucose (produced from starches and sugars) without oxygen, from glucose with oxygen, and from fats with oxygen. By far the most efficient method is with glucose and oxygen. Glucose without oxygen (anaerobic metabolism) can produce only 1/19 the amount of ATP that can be produced with an adequate oxygen supply. The muscle cells apparently cannot produce ATP from fats as fast as they can from glucose, and it requires more oxygen to do so. Therefore, the key to getting miles out of the legs lies in glucose storage and conservation. Almost all the glucose that is burned on a day's ride is already stored at the beginning of the day in the muscles as a polymer called glycogen.

The glycogen stores can be maximized by (1) good conditioning; (2) eating a high-carbohydrate diet and resting the muscles for three days prior to a race or long ride; (3) glycogen loading which includes a three-day period of exercise and low-carbohydrate diet followed by a three-day period of rest and a high-carbohydrate diet. I don't recommend this kind of low-carbohydrate diet for people over age 40 or for rides of less than 100 miles. It just isn't necessary.

A rider's maximum aerobic capacity is the amount of work he or she can do over a prolonged period of time without getting out of breath. At a work-expenditure rate of half or less of the maximum aerobic capacity (a nice, easy pace), about half the energy is supplied from fat and half from glucose. As the pace increases, the extra energy comes all from glucose, so that the glycogen will be used up after fewer miles have been traveled. When the glycogen is used up, the rider "hits the wall"—all metabolism comes from fat, the maximum work output goes way down, and the rider can even get hypoglycemia.

The tortoise knew he would have to call upon all his resources to win the big race. He exercised hard, but three days before the race he stopped training and began to eat a lot of sugars and starches. The morning of the race he took an easily digested, not-too-filling breakfast of toast and jelly. When the race began, he at first tried to keep up, but he was several hundred years older and knew he couldn't maintain the pace of the other rider. So he dropped back two gears until his legs were spinning easily, almost effortlessly. At every hill he was careful not to push. As he was riding a touring bike with a lot of low gears, he used these gears to maximum advantage to arrive at each hilltop without straining or breathlessness. On the way down, he did not coast, but continued a nice easy spin in a high gear, to keep his legs from getting stiff. He drank frequently from his water bottle which contained a diluted solution of one part commercial electrolyte solution to two parts water, and stopped to rest for about five minutes every two hours or so. After about eight hours, he passed a racing bike and a rider with long ears leaning against a tree. The hare never caught up—he had used up all his glycogen.

# Sensible Weight Loss

## David L. Smith, M.D.

If you are participating in the next Tour de France, or if you look like you spent your summer vacation in a POW camp, please skip this chapter. If you are like the rest of us overweight Americans, pedaling around hoping thereby to lose some weight, read on.

The Metropolitan Life Insurance Company has a certain vested interest in keeping its policyholders healthy. In the interest of not having to pay so much money out in life insurance claims, it has determined optimal weight ranges for the American population. People who exceed these weight limits, unless all the excess is due to an unusual amount of muscle, run an increased risk of developing various diseases, such as high blood pressure. Most Americans exceed these limits. (And don't claim a gland problem. Endocrine disorders leading to obesity are quite rare.) A more accurate method of measuring obesity can be performed by many internists through measuring the thickness of subcutaneous fat with a caliper.

The law of the conservation of energy holds just as rigidly for food and exercise as it does for anything else. If calories ingested exceed calories expended, pounds accumulate, and vice versa. Calories expended include a figure for the body heat maintenance, called the basal metabolic rate, and a figure for energy output. For the average sedentary American, these total about 2,000 to 2,500 calories per day.

Age is a factor too; as we get older our basal metabolic rate slowly declines. Also, most of us decrease our activity as we get older. Thus, our calories ingested must slowly decrease over the years or "fat and 40" will occur. After the age of 25 to 30, there is an inevitable slow loss of muscle and bone tissue even in fit people. The man who was in good condition at 25, and who stays in good condition for his age and keeps his weight the same, will nonetheless be relatively overweight at 50.

It has been said that it's almost impossible to lose weight by exercise alone, without *dieting*. This is true for short-term situations, because most people are unwilling to bicycle for an hour every time they eat a piece of chocolate cake, if they don't bicycle every day. However, frequent vigorous exercise expends a significant number of calories and is the real secret of weight control. A very sedentary desk worker may burn as few as 1,800 calories a day; a lumberjack can put out (and take in) three times as much. The average caloric expenditure of moderate bike riding has been estimated at 300 calories/hour. Thus a man who bicycles moderately for an hour daily (or who bicycles harder for a shorter period of time) can consume an extra 300 calories per day.

The regulatory center for the appetite is found in the hypothalamus, a part of the brain. Ideally, it regulates the caloric intake to be equal to the daily output. There are two reasons why this is often not the case. (1) People eat when they aren't really hungry, and keep eating after they have had enough, for either social or emotional reasons. (2) The lower limit of the regulatory capacity of the hypothalamus is about 2,500 calories; that means most people will be hungry with an intake less than 2,500 calories per day, even if output is only 2,000 calories or less. This is why dieting alone without exercise, is usually unsuccessful. Most people don't have the willpower to stay hungry all the time. People who get a moderate amount of exercise, expending over 2,500 calories a day, will eventually reach a normal weight without any caloric restriction, unless they eat when they aren't hungry.

There is an interesting phenomenon which takes place after a meal, called the "thermic" effect of food. This means that a certain percentage of the digested food is burned into heat directly by the intestine. Exercise immediately after a meal increases the amount of thermic effect, and therefore burns more calories up than a similar amount of exercise before a meal. However, I don't recommend a combination of a heavy meal followed by strenuous exercise; heat-fainting or sunstroke can ensue.

Many people are chronic crash dieters. They go on crash diets until they lose some weight, then gain it right back again when they go back to their old ways. Dieting is probably not worth doing if you can't keep the pounds off. Keeping it off involves getting in the habit of eating only enough to stave off the hunger pangs and exercising enough to keep the hypothalamus in balance.

Smoking tends to control weight, due to the appetite-supressing effect of nicotine. However, it is better to be fat than to smoke.

Diet pills, which are of various sorts, are either dangerous, and/or worthless, and/or habit forming. The same statement holds for fad diets, even those published by physicians, which are nutritionally grossly unbalanced. There is no substitute for willpower.

I can think of a lot more dietary rules, but the following are the most important:

1. Get at least 20 minutes of vigorous exercise, such as bicycling, every day, diet or no. This will maintain cardiovascular tone and prevent loss of muscle tissue.
2. Do not go into a complete fast. Start with a balanced 1,000- to 1,200-calorie diet, containing at least three ounces of lean meat per day, to help prevent breakdown of body protein (muscle). When your willpower to stay on the diet is gone, try not to ingest more than 2,500 calories per day until ideal body weight is reached.
3. The first three to five pounds of weight loss is mostly fluid and protein. Expect a three- to five-pound weight rebound when the diet is over.
4. Keep fat intake low, whether dieting or not. Fats are bad for the arteries and have a tremendously high calorie content per gram.
5. Weigh the portions of food until you are sure you can estimate the amount you take.

# Desirable Weights for Men and Women
# According to Height and Frame
# Ages 25 and Over*
# Weight in Pounds (in indoor clothing)

| Height (in shoes)† | Small Frame | Medium Frame | Large Frame |
|---|---|---|---|
| **Men** | | | |
| 5 ft.  2 in. | 112–120 | 118–129 | 126–141 |
| 5 ft.  3 in. | 115–123 | 121–133 | 129–144 |
| 5 ft.  4 in. | 118–126 | 124–136 | 132–148 |
| 5 ft.  5 in. | 121–129 | 127–139 | 135–152 |
| 5 ft.  6 in. | 124–133 | 130–143 | 138–156 |
| 5 ft.  7 in. | 128–137 | 134–147 | 142–161 |
| 5 ft.  8 in. | 132–141 | 138–152 | 147–166 |
| 5 ft.  9 in. | 136–145 | 142–156 | 151–170 |
| 5 ft. 10 in. | 140–150 | 146–160 | 155–174 |
| 5 ft. 11 in. | 144–154 | 150–165 | 159–179 |
| 6 ft.  0 in. | 148–158 | 154–170 | 164–184 |
| 6 ft.  1 in. | 152–162 | 158–175 | 168–189 |
| 6 ft.  2 in. | 156–167 | 162–180 | 173–194 |
| 6 ft.  3 in. | 160–171 | 167–185 | 177–199 |
| 6 ft.  4 in. | 164–175 | 172–190 | 182–204 |
| **Women** | | | |
| 4 ft. 10 in. | 92–98 | 96–107 | 104–119 |
| 4 ft. 11 in. | 94–101 | 98–110 | 106–122 |
| 5 ft.  0 in. | 96–104 | 101–113 | 109–124 |
| 5 ft.  1 in. | 99–107 | 104–116 | 112–128 |
| 5 ft.  2 in. | 102–110 | 107–119 | 115–131 |
| 5 ft.  3 in. | 105–113 | 110–122 | 118–134 |
| 5 ft.  4 in. | 108–116 | 113–126 | 121–138 |
| 5 ft.  5 in. | 111–119 | 116–130 | 125–142 |
| 5 ft.  6 in. | 114–123 | 120–135 | 129–146 |
| 5 ft.  7 in. | 118–127 | 124–139 | 133–150 |
| 5 ft.  8 in. | 122–131 | 128–143 | 137–154 |
| 5 ft.  9 in. | 126–135 | 132–147 | 141–158 |
| 5 ft. 10 in. | 130–140 | 136–151 | 145–163 |
| 5 ft. 11 in. | 134–144 | 140–155 | 149–168 |
| 6 ft.  0 in. | 138–148 | 144–159 | 153–174 |

*Prepared by the Metropolitan Life Insurance Company.
†One-inch heels for men and 2-inch heels for women.

# Training for the Long Ride

## David L. Smith, M.D.

The century, 100 miles in 12 hours, has been a test of cycling endurance for many years. Each September, League of American Wheelmen clubs all over the country sponsor centuries. I realize that there are plenty of young but seasoned riders who do not think a century very difficult unless it is done as a race, but to the novice or older cyclist it can be quite a formidable challenge.

The month of September is well chosen for a century. The cyclist has had the opportunity to train during the summer months, and there are still 12 hours of honest daylight daily until late in the month. The weather is more comfortable in most parts of the country than in July or August.

The training program that is outlined in this chapter will, I think, be sufficient to enable most cyclists to complete a century in 12 hours after two months. However, I realize that there may well be those who cannot increase their cycling capacity at the rate specified in the tables. A slower rate of increase should enable most of these cyclists to eventually build up their capacity to that which is needed. Most cycling enthusiasts will continue to build leg strength and endurance for several years before a maximum is reached, so if you are not able to do a century this year, you will be more likely to be able to do it next year, whatever your age.

The type of bicycle used is of some importance. Anybody who is a serious enough cyclist to want to ride centuries will probably want a pretty good bike. The following features are in my estimation very helpful.

A 10-speed or more, with a range of gearing wide enough to handle any anticipated conditions without too much stress and strain, is essential. For most cyclists, a gear range down into the low 30s will not be too low if hills or head winds are encountered. Tires should be 27 x 1¼ inch or narrower.

Dropped (racing or randonneur) handlebars require a crouched position which lessens wind resistance.

Toe clips and cleats will increase pedaling efficiency. Cycling shoes or an ordinary pair of leather shoes with laces can be used.

Wear a helmet, preferably the hard-shell-type helmet made especially for cycling. Several good brands are now on the market.

The tourist can and should carry more gear than the racer, especially for long rides. My list of essentials would include: tire pump, tool and tire patch kit, first-aid kit, identification and money, maps (as needed), a water-bottle capacity of a full quart (such as two 1-pint bottles), snack food, sunscreen and sunglasses, helmet- or glasses-mounted mirror, and dog repellent.

Except for the above, be ruthless in leaving things at home. You can do without fenders, kickstand, and handlebar mirror.

A good lightweight pair of wheels is well worth the investment. Rims should be alloy, with a tire that will take at least 85 pounds of pressure. The wind resistance of the tire is of some concern, because the top of the tire has a wind speed which is double that of the rest of the bike, and wind resistance increases proportionately to the square of the wind speed.

The following accessories can lessen either wind resistance or power-train losses: wind fairing (including the Edge and Zzipper); narrow chain (for example, the Ultra-6); ball-bearing derailleur pulleys (such as Bullseye).

Preparation of the bicycle is perhaps of more importance than buying wind fairings and the like. The bike should be clean and well lubricated. I prefer nondetergent motor oil for exposed surfaces, such as chain and derailleurs, and a good grade of lightweight grease for bearings. Sealed bearings require less maintenance but may have slightly more drag than nonsealed types.

A certain amount of preparation of the "motor" is also necessary. Men over 35 and women over 45 who are not accustomed to strenuous exercise, especially if they smoke or are overweight, should get a thorough physical exam and an exercise stress test (treadmill or bicycle ergometer), before beginning the training program. This may sound like a plot to enrich my fellow doctors, but men in their thirties can and do have heart attacks, and I figure it is better to be out some money than out your life. Other general rules followed by anyone in training would be the following: balanced diet, adequate rest, no tobacco, and no more than two drinks per day.

The training schedule (Table I) is divided into three general types of training: hard fast riding (Tuesdays and Thursdays) for muscle strength and aerobic conditioning, long but easier riding on Saturdays for endurance and pacing, and rest or light riding the rest of the week. There is nothing sacrosanct about doing it on these particular days of the week, but the table is arranged in this manner because I think that most people will have more time for a long ride

# Training Schedules

## Table I: Weeks 1 – 7

**Week 1**
Sunday–30 minutes
Monday–15 minutes
Tuesday–30 minutes
Wednesday–15 minutes
Thursday–30 minutes
Friday–15 minutes
Saturday–10 miles in 1 hour

**Week 2**
Sunday–rest
Monday–20 minutes
Tuesday–40 minutes
Wednesday–20 minutes
Thursday–40 minutes
Friday–20 minutes
Saturday–15 miles in 1½ hours

**Week 3**
Sunday–rest
Monday–25 minutes
Tuesday–50 minutes
Wednesday–25 minutes
Thursday–50 minutes
Friday–25 minutes
Saturday–20 miles in 2 hours

**Week 4**
Sunday–rest
Monday–30 minutes
Tuesday–60 minutes
Wednesday–30 minutes
Thursday–60 minutes
Friday–30 minutes
Saturday–30 miles in 3 hours

**Week 5**
Sunday–rest
Monday–35 minutes
Tuesday–70 minutes
Wednesday–35 minutes
Thursday–70 minutes
Friday–35 minutes
Saturday–45 miles in 4½ hours

**Week 6**
Sunday–rest
Monday–40 minutes
Tuesday–80 minutes
Wednesday–40 minutes
Thursday–80 minutes
Friday–40 minutes
Saturday–60 miles in 6 hours

**Week 7**
Sunday–rest
Monday–45 minutes
Tuesday–90 minutes
Wednesday–45 minutes
Thursday–90 minutes
Friday–45 minutes
Saturday–75 miles in 7½ hours

## Table II: Week 8

| Full Carbohydrate Loading | Modified Carbohydrate Loading |
|---|---|
| **Sunday**— exercise to exhaustion, then start Phase I diet | rest day; normal diet |
| **Monday**— exercise to exhaustion; continue Phase I diet | 90 minutes; normal diet |
| **Tuesday**— exercise to exhaustion; continue Phase I diet | 45 minutes; normal diet |
| **Wednesday**— exercise to exhaustion, then start Phase II diet | 90 minutes, then start Phase II diet |
| **Thursday**— rest day; Phase II diet | rest day; Phase II diet |
| **Friday**— rest day; Phase II diet | rest day; Phase II diet |
| **Saturday**— day of century ride | day of century ride |

on Saturday or Sunday. If you take some other day of the week off, do the long ride on that day and rearrange the schedule accordingly. However, keep in mind that hard and easy days should alternate, with one complete rest day per week. Most people holding regular jobs or going to school simply cannot ride for more than 1½ hours a day. Weekday training is therefore time limited rather than mileage limited. Saturday training rides are on a basis of both time and miles.

Observe these rules while following Table I:

The longer weekday workouts (Tuesday, Thursday) should be done as vigorously as possible and preferably without stopping. Some people may prefer to cycle by heart rate—the maximum heart rate averages 220 minus age in years—these rides should be done at 70 to 85 percent of maximum heart rate. On Saturday rides, you may stop as often as you want, as long as you complete the ride in the allotted time. An average 10 miles per hour will be maintained. The short workouts (Monday, Wednesday, Friday) can be at as easy a pace as desired.

If you have unusual difficulty with breathlessness, chest pain, or any unusual signs of fatigue other than a little leg soreness, see your doctor again before proceeding with the training. Unusual amounts of pain from any part of the body are a sign that you should back off for a while until your body can adapt.

Drink plenty of fluids, especially on the longer rides. Drink at least one pint per hour in hot weather; water and fruit drinks are best.

If you are already riding as much as is prescribed for Week 1, you may start directly with Week 2; if you are already at Week 2, start with Week 3, and so on through the schedule. But be honest about what you are already doing.

If you feel unusually fatigued at the end of your weekday rides so that you are not able to do your usual activities for the rest of the day, slow down a little. If you are unusually tired on your rest day or the day after, or if you are unable to complete the Saturday ride in the allotted time, do not proceed on to the next week. Instead, stay at the same level of training until you are feeling more fit; then proceed into the next week's training.

If you need to lose weight, by all means do so. But do not try to lose more than two pounds per week while in training.

The reader will note that Table I goes through only seven weeks. Training during the eighth week depends on the cyclist's health and general condition on completing the 75-mile ride. A cyclist under the age of 40 who feels quite fatigued after the 75-mile ride may elect to carbohydrate-load during the eighth week (Table II). A cyclist over 40, or one with any heart or circulatory disorder or elevated cholesterol or triglyceride levels, should do only the Modified Carbohydrate Loading. A cyclist who feels quite chipper after the 75 miles probably does not need the Full Carbohydrate-Loading diet but can elect to do Modified Carbohydrate Loading if desired. Modified Carbohydrate Loading is much more comfortable to do because it does not involve exercising to exhaustion on a low-carbohydrate diet during the first part of the week.

The Phase I diet is high in protein and fats; the Phase II diet is high in carbohydrates (Table III). The rationale behind this training method is that if the muscles are exercised and starved for carbohydrates, their preferred fuel, they will store more glycogen (a form of carbohydrate) during the rest days, and you will have more fuel to go farther on the century day. If you do only the Modified Carbohydrate-Loading program, the muscles will store more glycogen than usual but less than with the Full Carbohydrate-Loading program. The problem with the Full Carbohydrate-Loading program is that it is quite uncomfortable; the muscles will fatigue and tire after only a few miles of cycling, and you will not feel well during this sort of diet. Also the Phase I diet is high in cholesterol and saturated fats, which could be dangerous for someone with hardening of the arteries.

On the day of the ride, I recommend the following:

1.  The bike should be in top shape, freshly cleaned and oiled on Thursday and Friday rest days.

2.  Carry at least one quart of fluid water in one bottle and a mildly sweet beverage in the other. Drink plenty, at least one pint an hour. Avoid salty foods and beverages. Salt tablets are not recommended.

3.  Eat a Phase II breakfast, enough to satisfy hunger but not to feel stuffed.

4.  Consume high-carbohydrate foods during the ride and at the lunch stop. Carry fruit (bananas are a favorite) in your handlebar bag; eat as soon as you begin to feel hungry. Avoid salty junk foods.

5.  If time permits, rest an hour at the lunch stop. This will allow some digestion and muscle glycogen storage to take place. When you get back on the bike, you will feel stiff for a few miles, but then you will find that you have more energy and are doing much better than just before you stopped.

6.  Pace yourself. Ten miles in 55 minutes, rest 5 minutes, with an hour for lunch, will get you there with an hour to spare. On hills, gear way down so that you never exceed 50 percent of your maximum exercise capacity.

7.  One to two cups of coffee for breakfast, with a cup at lunch, may possibly help you go a little faster and easier, according to some recent research by Dr. David Costill. However, you will be making more frequent stops at the outhouse due to the action of caffeine on the kidneys, and you will have to drink more fluid to make up for this.

8.  Have someone waiting at the finish line who can shovel you into the car and drive you home.

# Training Schedules

## Table III: Phase I and II Diets*

### Food Groups and Daily Amounts

| | Phase I | Phase II |
|---|---|---|
| **Meat** | 20–25 ounces | 8 ounces |
| **Breads and Cereals** | up to 4 servings | up to 16 servings[†] |
| **Vegetables** | 3–4 servings | 3–4 servings[‡] |
| **Fruit** | up to 4 servings | up to 10 servings[§] |
| **Fats** | 8–9 ounces | 4–6 ounces |
| **Desserts** | 1–2 servings (only fruits and unsweetened gelatin) | up to 2 servings[‡] |
| **Beverages** | unlimited, but no sugar | unlimited |

[†](1 serving: 1 slice of bread or ½ cup cereal)
[‡](1 serving: ½ cup)
[§](1 serving: ½ cup or 1 piece of fruit)

*Modified from Nathan J. Smith, M.D. *Food for Sport.* Palo Alto, CA: Bull, 1976, pp. 82–3.

## Sample Meal Plans for Phase I and II Diets

| Phase I | Phase II |
|---|---|
| **Breakfast** | |
| 8 ounces unsweetened orange juice | 8 ounces unsweetened orange juice |
| 4 eggs | 2 slices toast with 2 teaspoons butter or jelly |
| 1 hamburger or homemade sausage patty | 1 cup cereal with low-fat milk |
| 1 slice toast (optional) | 1 egg (optional) |
| 4 teaspoons butter | |
| **Lunch** | |
| 1 meat sandwich (with butter or mayonnaise) | 1–2 sandwiches—each with 1 ounce meat or cheese, ½ teaspoon butter |
| 2–3 cheese sticks | 8 ounces low-fat milk |
| 1 tossed salad with oil dressing | 2 large bananas |
| 1 medium apple or orange (optional) | |

**Snacks**

1–2 meat sandwiches with butter
  1 cheese stick
  1 medium apple or
    banana (optional)

2 sandwiches—meat or
  nonmeat
1 serving fruit
8 ounces low-fat milk

**Dinner**

  10 ounces meat
  1 small baked potato, with
    2–3 teaspoons butter and
    1 tablespoon sour cream
  1 serving vegetable (no corn)
    with 1–2 teaspoons butter
  1 tossed salad
  1 small apple

4 ounces meat
1 medium baked potato with
  1 teaspoon butter
1 serving any vegetable
1–2 rolls, with 1 teaspoon butter
2 servings fruit
2 servings beverage, such as
  banana low-fat shake or
  unsweetened orange juice

# Training for Longevity

## David L. Smith, M.D.

I suspect that most physicians like people and need human contact. The ones who don't go into specialties where they can stay cloistered in a lab away from the press of the crowds. As much as we may love our patients, we often find them exasperating. Take, for instance, cyclists.

As much as we admonish them to stay home safely in bed, they insist on exposing themselves to the risk of falling off their bikes or even being hit by a truck, in order to get a little exercise to keep themselves healthy. Most cyclists seem to fear neither death nor injury. Or perhaps it is that we cyclists fear something else more—ill health and decrepitude. It is better to suffer a reparable injury, say a broken collarbone, than to have a massive heart attack and spend the rest of one's life in an enfeebled condition. If we all must go sometime, better to go suddenly and while having fun than a slow death after long suffering. Better to have a life of vigor, short or long, than one characterized by a long terminal period of decrepitude.

Of course, most of us are not going to be killed or crippled on the road if we are reasonably careful. But we fear that somehow our efforts will backfire. Jonathan Swift, in *Gulliver's Travels*, describes a mutant race of immortal men. This sounds most attractive, until he discovers that they get old just like anybody else. They spend the centuries miserably, more and more enfeebled but unable to die. Somehow we fear that if we take too good care of ourselves, this will happen to us. We will live long, but only our age will be prolonged.

Let me assure you that this has not been found to be the case. Active exercising people are granted the benefit of an active old age. Vigor is prolonged at the expense of the terminal stage. For most, active exercise like cycling will lead to a longer life span, and the extra years will be vigorous ones. There are many cyclists in their seventies, still vigorous and capable of long miles every day.

Athletic training has come a long way in the last 30 years. As training methods have been integrated with modern knowledge of body physiology, recorded times have continued to fall. If I wanted to make a very simplified list of some basic training principles for endurance sports, such as bicycle road racing, I would draw up the following:

1. Aerobic (distance) training to be emphasized, daily or on an every-other-day basis, with at least one rest day per week;
2. Sprinting and nonendurance activities perhaps once a week;
3. A balanced and complete diet, with emphasis on a relatively high-carbohydrate, low-fat calorie balance for maintenance of muscle glycogen stores. Protein content adequate but not excessive;
4. Adequate rest;
5. No tobacco, and little or no alcohol;
6. Careful weight control, body fat preferably 5 to 10 percent for men.

After making this list, it suddenly began to seem awfully familiar. Then it occurred to me that this is almost the same list that I might make as a recipe for longevity:

1. Aerobic (distance) training on a regular, everyday or every-other-day basis, for a minimum of 20 minutes per session;
2. At least one rest day per week;
3. A balanced and complete diet, with emphasis away from cholesterol and saturated fats, and with plenty of fiber, and a minimum of salt;
4. Adequate rest;
5. No tobacco, and little or no alcohol;
6. Careful weight control.

Now it seems to me that to be constantly in athletic training for some event or another might be the best way to stay motivated to continue a healthy life-style. If I'm looking forward to a century ride, long tour, or race, then I will be motivated to get in some training. A succession of upcoming events and always looking forward to the next one will keep me fit and healthy for a lifetime. If I don't deliberately commit myself for some big events then my motivation is soon gone, and flabbiness sets in.

For this reason, I think that cycle touring is the best thing to come along since the pneumatic tire. With such organizations as the International Bicycle Touring Society, the League of American Wheelmen, and Bikecentennial leading the way, the long-distance tour is becoming increasingly popular and offers the nonracer an ideal way to get and stay in shape. The next best things to come along are the Veterans, Masters, and Grand Masters racing categories. We old guys can race to our hearts' content without trying to compete against the young whippersnappers.

# Cycling and Aging

### David L. Smith, M.D.

Drs. Per-Olaf and Irma Astrand in Stockholm have done some very applicable work in studying the aerobic performance of individuals of different ages. Studying active, fit individuals, not necessarily super athletes, they found that peak performances for men were in the early twenties and by the age of 25, a 6 percent loss in performance had already occurred (measured on a bicycle ergometer). The decline in performance for women apparently did not begin until after 25, but performances for both men and women of different ages are so close on a percentage basis that the data for both can be combined. The table on the facing page is modified from their data.

This averages out to about 0.8 percent loss per year after age 20, over a lifetime. Percentage of aerobic capacity remaining equals 100 percent times 0.8 (age minus 20). However, declines are comparatively sharper in the earlier years than in the later ones. Of course, this says nothing about the amount of aerobic capacity of any one individual. A 64-year-old rider who has always had great athletic ability may still have more aerobic capacity than a less well-endowed 20-year-old.

## Age and Aerobic Performance

| Age | Percent of Aerobic Capacity Remaining |
|-----|---------------------------------------|
| 20  | 100 |
| 25  | 97  |
| 30  | 89  |
| 35  | 84  |
| 40  | 79  |
| 45  | 75  |
| 50  | 71  |
| 55  | 68  |
| 60  | 65  |
| 65  | 62  |
| 70  | 59  |

As a runner ages, this slowdown is painfully obvious. If a runner peaks in his/her twenties with a distance running speed of 10 miles per hour, this will be decreased to a little over 6½ miles per hour by age 60. However, the older cyclist riding in flat country has the advantage of disproportionate wind resistance. Because the power required to overcome wind resistance increases with the cube of the speed, it takes more power to go faster. Conversely, a considerable loss in power results in a comparatively modest drop in speed.

Now just for fun let's assume that you, while in your early twenties, were or are able to do a 25-mile time trial in exactly 1 hour. The table on page 38 is compiled from data published in *DeLong's Guide to Bicycles and Bicycling* (Radnor, PA: Chilton, 1974).

The time-trial record for 70-year-old men is not available, but veteran cyclist Ed Delano's time in 1977 was 1 hour, 16 minutes. He is in his early seventies and that time is rated as one of the best for his age. Why is the calculation 6 minutes shorter than his actual performance? One explanation is perhaps the paucity of competitors in this age group. Most 75-year-old persons are no longer athletically active. In 1977 Paul Deem, an Olympic racer, rode 25 miles in a little under 56 minutes. Perhaps when he is 70 he will set a new record.

All of the figures assume a flat course, which is typical of a time trial. On the hills, however, the slower cyclist will tend to fall behind because the wind-resistance advantage is lost. On a 10 percent grade, our 20-year-old cyclist with the 0.45 horsepower output will (using DeLong's data) climb at 10 miles per hour, while a 70-year-old

## Time Trials and the Effects of Aging

| Age | Horsepower Output | Speed (mph) | Time for 25 Miles* (hours: minutes) |
|---|---|---|---|
| 20 | 0.45 | 25 | 1:0 |
| 30 | 0.40 | 24 | 1:2.5 |
| 35 | 0.38 | 23.6 | 1:3.5 |
| 40 | 0.36 | 23.2 | 1:4.5 |
| 45 | 0.34 | 22.8 | 1:6 |
| 50 | 0.32 | 22.4 | 1:7 |
| 55 | 0.306 | 22.1 | 1:8 |
| 60 | 0.29 | 21.8 | 1:9 |
| 65 | 0.28 | 21.6 | 1:9.5 |
| 70 | 0.27 | 21.4 | 1:10 |

*Rounded off to the nearest ½ minute.

compatriot with an output of 0.27 horsepower will have slowed to 6 miles per hour, or little over half the speed of the younger rider.

From the point of view of gearing, this means that the top gear of the older cyclist will drop little, whereas the bottom gear will drop a great deal. Our younger rider might turn a gear of 95 on the level with a cadence of about 90 and a speed of 25 miles per hour; on a 10 percent grade with the same cadence, the cyclist would climb at 10 miles per hour with a gear of about 40. The older cyclist, assuming a cadence of 90, would use a gear of 80 on the level at a speed of 21½ miles per hour and gear in the low 20s on the upgrade at 6 miles per hour. (The percentage difference from 25 to 40 is much greater than the difference from 80 to 95.) Of course, as the gear range is thus widened, more gears must be added and the steps between gears must also be wider. The older cyclist who is lowering gears should seriously consider using 12- or 15-speed gearing in order to avoid undesirably wide gaps between gears.

What philosophical conclusion can be drawn from all this speculation? The conclusion is that cycling is an ideal lifetime exercise for both athlete and nonathlete. Even those with relatively low power outputs will make good time on level terrain, and thanks to modern-day, wide-range gearing with gears descending into the low 20s, the reasonably fit septuagenarian can climb steep grades without straining or getting off and walking.

# Carbohydrate Loading

## David L. Smith, M.D.

Carbohydrate loading was originally discovered by Swedish physicians studying performance of cross-country skiers. Cross-country skiers put out an enormous amount of energy—up to 6,500 calories per day—and need all the fuel they can get. (Incidentally, this is an excellent winter exercise for cyclists.) These and other researchers have found out that there are two kinds of muscle fibers: fast-contracting (sugar-burning) fibers and slow-acting (fat-burning) fibers. The fast-contracting fibers do most of the work until their supply of glycogen (a storage form of glucose) is used up. Then the slow-acting fibers have to do most of the work, and a noticeable drop in output often occurs.

A cyclist pedaling at 65 to 80 percent of his or her maximum output (going pretty fast) will use up glycogen stores in 1½ to 3 hours. If there were a way to increase the glycogen supply stored in the fast-acting fibers, a noticeable improvement in performance after this time could be expected. Carbohydrate loading is just such a way. The "full course" carbohydrate-loading technique consists of the following steps (see Table III: Phase I and II Diets in the previous chapter for dietary plan):

Day 1: The cyclist exhausts glycogen stores with a long, hard, exhausting ride (e.g., 50 to 100 miles depending on rider and terrain).

Days 1–3: The cyclist keeps fast-acting fibers depleted of glycogen by taking in a very low-carbohydrate diet (correspondingly high in fat), combined with continued hard training rides. During this time, the fast-acting fibers will increase their capability of taking in glucose when it does become available. Also, the fat-burning fibers will get a good workout.

Days 4–6: High-carbohydrate diet combined with rest enables the fast-acting fibers to store up as much as a double supply of glycogen.

Day 7: The big race (or double century)—high liquid intake before, during, and after the event. Generous amounts of sugar intake permitted up to 1½ hours before the event. During event, a drink containing not more than 2½ percent glucose (or other sugar) should be generously consumed.

Dr. Nathan J. Smith is the author of *Food for Sport* (Palo Alto, CA: Bull, 1976), which is the best book I have seen on nutrition for the athlete. He has granted permission to reprint the suggested diets above.

There are several problems associated with this technique:

1. The days without carbohydrates are pretty rough for most people. Believe me, you will feel lousy on Days 2–3, and your exercise capacity will be considerably reduced. Attempts to continue exercising to your usual tolerance can result in muscle and even kidney damage, especially if potassium and fluid intake have been low.
2. This diet is not for those with diabetes, arteriosclerosis, or other metabolic diseases requiring prescribed diets. It could at least theoretically lead to heart attacks or ketoacidosis (accumulation of acid of the body) in these people.
3. There are a few people with rare muscle-enzyme deficiencies who can develop muscle and kidney damage. A person with abnormally low exercise tolerance or who develops repeated cramps with moderate exercise may have this kind of a problem.
4. Alcohol is forbidden. I don't know of any better way to damage the liver than a high-fat, low-carbohydrate diet combined with John Barleycorn.
5. Carbohydrate loading is no substitute for training. You cannot sit on your can all summer and then do a double century in the fall with carbohydrate loading. The diet will not work for those whose muscles are in too poor a shape to make use of the extra fuel supply.
6. Don't use a big race to try the technique out for the first time. If for some reason you can't tolerate it, you will do less well than if you had not used it.
7. Overweight people will do better to reduce (by dieting with exercise) than relying on carbohydrate loading. Serious cyclists should aim for a 5 to 7 percent body-fat content, as measured by skinfold calipers or body plethysmography (this is thin). If by the week before the race you are still overweight, you can modify Phase I by eliminating the butter, sour cream, oil dressing, and sausage. (Burn your own fat instead.)
8. People over 40, who have not had a long-term commitment to physical fitness, may have an increased risk of heart attack or

muscle damage using the Full Carbohydrate-Loading diet. These people should follow carefully the dietary recommendations of the American Heart Association, and should not engage in strenuous competition without a thorough medical evaluation and physical-fitness training.

9. A high fluid intake is highly desirable throughout, and may make Phase I more comfortable.

If for some reason the Full Carbohydrate-Loading diet is impractical or dangerous for you, simply loading up on carbohydrates for about three days before the event can still be of benefit. If you are taking a tour of several days' duration, increasing your carbohydrate intake at meals and avoiding an unusually high fat intake, will keep you operating at peak efficiency.

# Caffeine, Alcohol, and Aspirin

## David L. Smith, M.D.

There have been some interesting ideas circulating in running circles recently that deserve some medical comments on these pages. The first are some recent studies about caffeine, which is commonly found in coffee, tea, and cola drinks and can be bought in pills such as Nodoz. Researchers have found that the amount of caffeine contained in one to two cups of coffee will increase the blood levels of free fatty acids, which can be used by the muscles for fuel. It has been suggested that small runners should take one and large runners two cups of coffee before a long run.

Be this as it may, it is also true that many doctors mistrust caffeine. It's just too much like an amphetamine for comfort. It's known to raise resting heart rate, can cause minor heart arrhythmias, and keeps people awake when they should be sleeping. It's been suspected but not proven that a high coffee intake could predispose drinkers to heart attacks.

Now I'm not as pure as the driven snow—I drink a lot of coffee—but if you don't drink coffee, please don't start using it just to get your free fatty acids up.

Fuel delivery to the muscles is just as much of a problem for the long-distance cyclist as it is for the long-distance runner. Dr. George

Sheehan, a noted authority on running, has suggested that runners drink beer as they go, in hopes that the alcohol could be used for fuel. At first, this didn't sound sensible to me. But on second thought, it didn't seem like such an absurd thing for him to say. Dr. Sheehan is a competitive runner. If his opponents drink enough beer, he will win. The fact is that the principal fuel for the muscles is glucose, part of which is supplied by the liver. Alcohol coming to the liver from the intestines disrupts many of its metabolic processes and lowers glucose output. Power output and straight riding are interfered with. Don't put a beer bottle in your water-bottle carrier, even if it fits. If you want some fuel as you ride, try making up a dilute (2½ percent is suggested) sugar solution with honey.

Aspirin has received a lot of medical and lay attention recently. It has many interesting effects on the body, one of which is to disrupt the function of blood platelets. Platelets are little bits of cellular material floating in the bloodstream whose function is to clump together during the formation of blood clots. As little as one aspirin will have a slight but definite effect against blood clotting for as long as a week.

In some cases, this is fine. Aspirin has been shown to help prevent the occurrence of certain types of strokes caused by the clotting of blood in the vessels supplying the brain, and may possibly help prevent heart attacks for the same reason, although there isn't proven evidence on this yet. However, a cyclist who has fallen on the head is more in danger of bleeding inside the head (a serious injury) than of clots in the blood vessels. Aspirin makes bleeding inside the head worse. For this reason I think cyclists, especially those too stubborn to wear a helmet, should stay away from aspirin unless it is being taken per a doctor's advice. If you hurt, take acetaminophen (such as Tylenol and Datril) instead. Better yet, grin and bear it.

# Food to Eat before the Tour

## Anita Hirsch

Before beginning a tour, it would be wise to know the best foods to eat. Of the three major nutrients we extract from foods, the carbohydrates are the ones most efficient for producing energy over the long haul. When using your muscles and pedaling, it is the carbohydrates that burn for energy. Carbohydrates are stored in the muscles and in the liver in the form of glycogen. In order to prevent depletion of glycogen stores, it is important to eat carbohydrate foods before the ride as well as during the ride. This is why professional cyclists, while training, carry rice cakes with them. Rice is a high-carbohydrate, easily digested food.

Other high-carbohydrate foods are those containing grains such as breads, pancakes, waffles, spaghetti, noodles, and cereals, especially oatmeal, white and sweet potatoes, parsnips, beets, corn, peas, and squash, and fruits such as bananas, apples, and dried fruits.

Fat also provides energy during exercise, especially during prolonged exercise such as touring. This fat should not be consumed directly before the tour, however, because fats remain in the stomach too long and give an undesirably full feeling. For this reason, greasy, fried foods should be avoided.

Protein, the last of the three major nutrients in food, is important for replacing body cells and increasing muscle mass. Once enough protein is eaten, any excess consumed is converted to carbohydrates or body fats.

Protein is not necessary for energy demands, but it is important because some amino acids are needed in changing carbohydrates and fats to energy. Protein needs of the body can be met with a normal food intake. In order to calculate protein needs, multiply body weight by 0.39. A cyclist weighing 150 pounds times 0.39 would need 58.5 grams of protein per day.

If the protein is eventually to be used for energy, don't consume too much protein by taking protein supplements or eating large amounts of meat. A person can only eat so much food; by eating too much protein one cannot eat enough of the fats and carbohydrates needed for energy. Too much protein will induce dehydration, loss of appetite, and diarrhea. Since extra amounts of water are needed to metabolize protein, too much protein consumed before a tour is not recommended.

Pretour, large, heavy meals should be eaten no sooner than three hours before beginning. This ensures the food will be out of the stomach before starting the tour.

Cyclists who are preparing for the Tour de France or the European Classics immediately before beginning a race consume a bottle of 440 grams (about 2 cups) of tea containing the juice of one lemon, honey, potassium, and sodium; five to six pieces of rice cake; biscuits; apple tarts; and dried fruits (figs and apricots).

These foods generally follow the pretour dietary practices as suggested before. In general, these practices are to eat foods high in carbohydrates directly before a tour. The food chosen should be such that hunger or weakness will not occur while riding.

It is upsetting during a ride to have to stop for urinary or bowel functions; therefore, avoid large amounts of protein, and bulky or high fiber or highly spiced foods immediately before starting out.

Before, during, and after riding, adequate amounts of liquids should be consumed. The best beverages are fruit drinks or water.

Foods eaten before riding should be familiar foods that have previously been consumed and agree with the system. Foods that cause flatulence or excess gas should be avoided.

Some cyclists report that the following foods give their stomachs an uncomfortable, full feeling: raw fruits and vegetables (salads), dried fruits, nuts, and whole-grain cereal products. Most cyclists also avoid milk and milk products because of the excess mucus formed in the throat.

In *The Complete Diet Guide for Runners and Other Athletes* by the editors of *Runner's World* (Mountain View, CA: 1978), Ellington Darden, Ph.D., suggests that too much honey eaten before an event will draw fluids from all parts of the body into the gastrointestinal tract. This shift could cause dehydration at the time when fluids are important. Cramps, nausea, bloated stomach, and diarrhea can occur when too much sugar is consumed.

Below are four natural pretour snack recipes.

# Scotch Broth

1 pound stewing beef or neck of mutton, with fat trimmed off
1 shinbone
3 quarts cold water
4 peppercorns
1 bay leaf
salt to taste (optional)
½ cup barley
3 carrots, diced
1 turnip, diced
1 medium-size onion, diced
chopped parsley for garnish

Wipe the meat and shinbone and put into large pot with 3 quarts of cold water. Bring to boil; add peppercorns, bay leaf, salt, and barley; reduce heat and simmer without boiling for 1 hour.

After meat stock has simmered for an hour, add vegetables and simmer until vegetables are tender (about 1 hour). When broth is ready, the meat can be taken out, cut into small pieces, and returned to the soup.

Serve with parsley as a garnish. Yields about 12 cups.

from *The Rodale Cookbook*
by Nancy Albright

# Oatmeal Crackers

1½ cups oatmeal (ground to a coarse flour in electric blender)
1 cup whole wheat flour
½ teaspoon salt (optional)
½ cup water
5 tablespoons oil
1 tablespoon honey

Preheat oven to 350°F.

Combine dry ingredients. Combine water, oil, and honey. Stir dry ingredients into wet ones to make a cohesive ball.

Butter cookie sheet and pat out dough in shape of pan. Roll to thickness of ⅛ inch using rolling pin. Score with knife in desired shapes and bake 12 minutes in preheated oven. Cool 5 minutes before removing crackers from cookie sheet. Yields 4 dozen, 2-inch-square crackers.

from *Rodale's Naturally Great Foods Cookbook*
by Nancy Albright

# Carrot Yogurt Squares

3  cups whole wheat flour
2  teaspoons baking soda
1  teaspoon baking powder
1  teaspoon salt (optional)
1  teaspoon fresh-grated lemon peel
1  cup (8 ounces) plain yogurt
1  cup grated carrots
¾  cup honey
½  cup chopped nuts
½  cup seedless raisins
2  eggs
⅓  cup oil
¼  cup milk

Preheat oven to 350°F.

Stir together dry ingredients. Mix together remaining ingredients.

Add liquid to dry ingredients, stirring only until flour is moistened. Spread in greased 9x13-inch baking pan.

Bake in a preheated oven for 30 to 35 minutes. Cool and cut into squares. Yields about 30 squares.

Jean M. Lawn
Providence, RI

# Apricot—Raisin Cookies

1 cup seedless raisins
1 cup dried apricots
3 tablespoons water
1 cup whole wheat flour
½ cup non-fat dry milk
½ cup wheat germ
¼ teaspoon baking powder
¼ teaspoon baking soda
½ cup butter
½ cup peanut butter
½ cup honey
1 teaspoon vanilla
1 egg, beaten
3 tablespoons water
½ cup unsalted sunflower seeds or nuts
1 cup oatmeal, uncooked

Preheat oven to 375°F.

Chop or cut raisins and apricots coarsely. Put in saucepan with 3 tablespoons of water and cook until fruits are moist (about 2 minutes). Set aside.

Combine whole wheat flour, dry milk, wheat germ, baking powder, and baking soda.

Cream butter and peanut butter until soft. Add honey and beat until soft. Add vanilla and egg. Beat well. Add flour mixture slowly, alternating with water. Stir in sunflower seeds (or nuts), oatmeal, and fruit mixture.

Place heaping tablespoons of dough on greased baking sheet and spread to 2-inch circles.

Bake in a preheated oven about 10 minutes, then remove to wire racks to cool. Makes about 3 dozen cookies.

Kathleen Dunstan
Cuyahoga Falls, OH

# Fluid and Mineral Replacement for the Cyclist

## Anita Hirsch

When you are hot and thirsty, there is nothing like a cold drink to refresh you. Water is still the best and all-time favorite. Sometimes we get so wrapped up in what kind of drink to buy or prepare that we forget about the benefits of clear, cold water.

It is most important to replace the water from sweat loss. In comparison to the mineral salts lost in perspiration, the water loss is greater and should be replaced quickly. Perspiring is a necessary function that cools the body when it is hot. The more perspiration lost without replacement, the higher the body temperature will go, eventually reaching a critical level and resulting in heat stroke.

To check on how much water you lose during exercise, weigh youself before and after exercising and you will know how much water you should replace. If you lost one pound, you will have to replace it with one pint or two cups of water. Ordinarily about one quart of liquid intake a day is enough to maintain water balance, but if you are active, more must be consumed.

Water is also contained in many of the solid foods we eat. For example, tomatoes, leafy greens, melons, and strawberries hold about 90 percent water. This water also contributes to your fluid intake.

The general feeling as far as replacing salt or sodium is that the amount normally found in foods is enough to replace that lost in perspiration. If you lose over six pounds immediately after exercise, then salt tablets would be necessary (Jane Voichick, Ph.D.; and Peter Hanson, M.D.) "Nutrition for Performance." *Professional Nutritionist.* vol. 10 (1978): 1–3.

The dietary need for sodium and potassium is almost the same; therefore, if you take salt tablets you don't get enough potassium. The intake of potassium and sodium has a delicate balance that must be maintained.

Sodium is necessary to maintain the shift of water through the cells from one part of the body to another. This mineral aids in the transfer of water-soluble substances, including nutrients and glucose through the cells. It helps regulate the acid—base balance of the blood.

Foods that are high in protein are generally high in sodium content. Examples are meat, poultry, fish, seafood, eggs, milk, and cheeses. All baked goods made with baking powder and baking soda are high in sodium. Most commercially processed foods contain added salt.

Potassium plays an important part in muscle and nerve responses, in maintaining the normal rhythm of the heart, and in intracellular fluid balance. Too much potassium is not good. Potassium salts can cause ulcers because they are irritating to the gastrointestinal tract.

Foods high in potassium are bananas; apricots; oranges; canteloupes; coconuts; brewer's yeast; dried peas, beans, lentils, and soybeans; molasses (especially blackstrap molasses); peanuts; wheat germ; dried fruits, such as raisins, apricots, and peaches; and tomato juice. Many cyclists carry and eat plenty of raisins and other dried fruits for their potassium content.

This is preferable to taking medicinal potassium supplements, which "are generally unpalatable, require a physician's prescription, and may be harmful to healthy individuals." (Helen W. Lane, Ph.D., R.D.; and James J. Cerda, M.D. "Potassium Requirements and Exercise." *Journal of the American Dietetic Association.* July 1978, pp. 54–55). (Potassium supplements are obtainable in natural food stores, but in dosages of not more than 100 milligrams per tablet.) Indeed, overuse of potassium chloride, sometimes called potassium salt, has been known to be fatal.

Drinks made with orange or apricot juices would be good thirst quenchers as well as high in needed potassium. Here are two drink recipes that are easily made and carried:

# Orange Quencher

⅓  cup fresh-squeezed orange juice
⅔  cup water
1  teaspoon honey
pinch of salt (optional)

Combine above ingredients. Makes 1 cup.

## Golden Punch

1  cup fresh apple juice
½  cup fresh apricot nectar
½  cup fresh-squeezed orange juice
½  cup ice water or ice cubes

Stir the juices together and pour over ice in Thermos bottle. Makes 2½ cups.

# Medical Q and A

I am a male, 34; of average bone structure; and 6 feet, 3 inches tall in my bare feet. How much should I weigh to maximize my performance as a bike racer with an emphasis on hill climbing?

I have read that long-distance runners should weigh 20 percent less than average. Average for me is 193; 20 percent less is 155. Does this reduction percentage hold true for cyclists as well as long-distance runners?

W. L., Boulder, CO

*The answer to your question is not so simple as it may sound. A change in weight can be due to a change in body-fat content, muscle content, or both. The percentage of body fat can be estimated very closely by the procedure of body plethysmography (determining variations in the size of an organ or limb and in the amount of blood present), and somewhat less accurately by the use of skinfold calipers. Body plethysmograph equipment is available at universities with extensive exercise physiology labs; skinfold calipers are less expensive and are being increasingly used by coaches and doctors, especially those specializing in sports medicine or the treatment of obesity.*

*Long-distance runners are very thin (ectomorphic); they lack body fat (7 percent or less of total body weight in good marathoners), but also lack muscle bulk. Bike racers appear to have more musculature (they are more mesomorphic), but I know of no reason why a cyclist would need more than 7 percent body fat.*

*My answer to you is to try to bring your body-fat content down to 7 percent or less, concurrently with a training program to improve your muscular capacity to a maximum.*

David L. Smith, M.D.

My husband and I are planning a two-week bicycle trip. We will be traveling the southwestern area of Colorado. Our problem is that we are both vegetarians (no meat, fish, or eggs) and are concerned about our diet for the trip. I really feel we'll need something substantial to keep up with an average pace of 50 to 60 miles per day. We want to keep our load as light as possible. Could you please give us some healthful eating tips?

D. H., Denver, CO

*I don't think you will have any trouble finding enough energy from vegetarian sources. Vegetarian foods are high in carbohydrates, which are just what you will need for a long day's ride. You can get plenty from such products as milk, grains, and fruits. I'd suggest allowing at least 4,000 calories a day.*

*Your protein requirements may be a bigger problem. I'd advise allowing at least 1 gram/kilogram or 0.45 gram/pound of body weight per day. Newer research indicates that if protein of high quality is available (meat, milk, and eggs, or a very judicious vegetarian diet), the actual minimal requirements, if no body-building is going on, will be somewhat less. My suggestion for body-builders and racers would be to continue at the old requirement of 0.45 gram/pound. I think 100 grams a day is probably excessive. As you probably know, you have three basic protein sources to choose from: legumes; grains, nuts, seeds; and dairy products. The first two groups should always be eaten together or with dairy products to obtain a complete mixture of amino acids. Most of your protein and fat should be taken at the evening meal, with breakfast, lunch, and snacks being mostly carbohydrate.*

*You didn't say whether you'd be camping all the way or eating in restaurants. In any case, you should consider carrying freeze-dried or dehydrated foods with you. The R.E.I. Co-op, 1525 Eleventh Avenue, Seattle, WA 98201, mail-orders a large number of dried foods including vegetarian meals. If you're interested in making your own dehydrated food, there is a paperback book, Dry It You'll Like It (MacManiman, Gen. Billing, MT: Montana Readings, 1974) for $3.95.*

David L. Smith, M.D.

I do a lot of touring and to provide energy I munch on raisins.

My brother wrestles on the high school wrestling team. His coach tells him to eat honey before a match. I'd like to know if honey provides instant energy? If so, why don't racers eat honey?

B. W., Cicero, IL

*After several hours of riding, the leg muscles become depleted of glycogen, a storage form of sugar. At that point they must switch to burning fat. The effect of this on riding, for most people, is equivalent to putting kerosene in the gas tank. You can still go but not very well. Eating honey will delay the glycogen depletion a little. But while strenuous exercise is going on, the intestines have a very limited capacity to digest. Every rider has his or her own preferences, but I understand that in the long races the pros do eat on the road, consuming high-carbohydrate foods such as bananas. In addition, highly trained endurance athletes can burn fat with almost the same efficiency as glycogen.*

*Glycogen-loading techniques, or simply a high-carbohydrate diet while on tour, will help to keep the muscles full of readily available glycogen.*

David L. Smith, M.D.

I have recently been using one of the electrolyte-replacement beverages with completely favorable results but would appreciate answers to the following questions:

1. I consume about one pint for 30 miles of biking in 80°F. weather. Is there an upper limit on consumption, or is thirst a satisfactory guide?
2. Should some people not use these products?

J. D. M., Old Greenwich, CT

1. *For people with normal kidneys, thirst is a fairly satisfactory guide but tends to lag behind actual water loss. Water replacement is of the first importance. Excess electrolytes will be excreted in the urine.*
2. *People with hypertension and/or kidney disease should be wary of these products. Severely damaged kidneys are unable to adequately excrete salt which, therefore, accumulates in the blood and must be diluted with retained water. The resulting increase in blood volume is a common cause of hypertension.*

Eugene A. Gaston, M.D.

You once suggested that a person with a case of hypertension partake of Gatorade, a drink which is not recommended for people with high blood pressure or diabetes.

My mother and my brother-in-law have had high blood pressure but are now diabetics. For their high blood pressure they kept a supply of bananas for potassium and oranges for liquid, body salts, and acids. For the water bottle may I suggest Bananamel, a soymeal product rich in potassium, sold at natural food stores? Is Bananamel a good source of potassium?

M. K., McAlester, OK

*Gatorade, as with other electrolyte solutions, contains salt. Too much salt is definitely contraindicated for high blood pressure, but a certain amount of salt intake is necessary for life.*

*Diabetics have a similar problem: they need to take in a certain amount of sugar, especially if exercising, but the sugar intake must be regulated. There is no way I can substitute for the advice of the patient's own doctor in regard to how much of these substances they should ingest.*

*Both bananas and oranges are good sources of potassium, but they are also excellent sources of carbohydrates (sugar) as well and should therefore not be eaten in unlimited quantities by a diabetic. I haven't had any experience with Bananamel; we don't have a natural food store here in the little town where I live. There are several prescription elixirs and tablets on the market that are potassium supplements.*

David L. Smith, M.D.

We are cycling vegetarians. Can you recommend any books on food and health?

G. L., Stow, OH

*I would recommend one or more of the following for your reading:*

1. *Goodhart, R. S., and Shils, M. E. Modern Nutrition in Health and Disease: Dietotherapy. Philadelphia: Lea and Febiger, 1973.*
2. *National Research Council, Food and Nutrition Board. Recommended Dietary Allowances. 8th ed. Washington, DC: National Academy of Sciences, 1974.*
3. *Turner, Dorothea. Handbook of Diet Therapy. 5th ed. Chicago: University of Chicago Press, 1970.*
4. *National Research Council, Food and Nutrition Board, Committee on Amino Acids. Evaluation of Protein Nutrition. Washington, DC: National Academy of Sciences, 1959.*

David L. Smith, M.D.

**Get Fit with Bicycling**

I'm 16 years of age; am 6 feet, 2 inches tall; weigh 157 pounds; and love to ride in the country. About one month ago I was on a short ride when my legs gave out. I could not even hold myself up when I stopped. I lay in a ditch for about an hour until I saw a car and waved it down. They took me back to town. Since then, even short rides make my legs and ankles weak. What could be causing this? It comes on without warning, but I get very tired just before it happens.

N. S., Greenville, OH


*It sounds to me as if you are running out of gas. The chief source of fuel for the muscles during exercise is glucose, which is stored in the muscles and liver as glycogen. The muscles can work at a reduced rate on other fuels such as fatty acids from fat stores. With your slight build it doesn't sound like you carry around large reserves of any of these fuels. I think that if you increase your carbohydrate (sugar and starch) intake before and during your rides, you will regain your former capabilities. This means bananas, oranges, orange juice, bread, and the like. Sometimes a salt or other electrolyte deficiency produces similar symptoms. Try drinking an electrolyte solution such as ERG or Gatorade instead of plain water as you ride. This will supply electrolytes and sugar. If my suggestions don't help, see your doctor.*

David L. Smith, M.D.


I have a series of questions about the contribution of biking to losing weight. I am a 27-year-old woman, 5 feet, 3 inches; weight, 112 pounds. My ideal weight is somewhere between 106 and 108 pounds. For the past three weeks I have been riding from 12 to 15 miles every day. I ride in an 82-inch gear with a cadence of approximately 75 to 80 revolutions per minute.

I would like to be able to calculate the approximate number of calories I burn by biking, but various formulas are vague and vary a great deal. For example, one formula states that a person burns approximately 600 calories per hour if biking hard. Is there a formula that is more specific that could be based on a person's size and the speed at which one is biking?

My purpose for writing is to ask why you think I am not losing weight. I have been on a 1,000-calorie diet that is high protein and low carbohydrate. For example, the diet consists of lean beef and fish, yogurt (plain), dry-flake cottage cheese, low-fat cheese, and egg whites. I have lost about three pounds, but now I am retaining water. Even with the water retention, I would expect to lose more weight than I have.

I am aware of the dangers of this kind of diet, but I do want to lose the extra pounds. I have been feeling fine, I have energy, and my muscle tone has improved greatly since I started riding this summer. If you have any advice on how I can change the diet to speed up the weight loss, I would appreciate it.

B. E., San Diego, CA

*I'm glad I'm not trying to keep up with you. It sounds as if you are in excellent physical condition, and for that reason my advice is not to worry about losing any more weight at the present. That's because most charts of ideal weights don't take into account the amount of muscle mass a fit person will have. You should instead go by skinfold-caliper measurements to estimate the amount of adipose fat present. I would guess that you probably don't have any extra fat.*

*The amount of energy expended is indeed a slippery measurement, and I doubt that I can come up with any better formula than you already have. There are just too many variables to put it all in one formula. An average 150-pound racing cyclist traveling at 19 mph, which is about what you are doing, would expend 10.5 calories per minute; you may be expending a little less since you are light, but I would say that you would be expending at least 500 calories per hour. In any case, I do not think your lack of weight loss is due to loafing.*

*I can think of several reasons why you may not be losing any more weight. In the first place, a lot of people who think they are on a 1,000-calorie diet are really taking in a lot more because they do not weigh out their portions. The portions on those diet sheets, when weighed out, usually look like starvation rations.*

*Second, water retention can mask several pounds of weight loss, or conversely, a lot of water loss can make it look as if the diet is working even better than expected.*

*Third, the body has a remarkable capacity to conserve energy during dieting, to the extent of even altering the basal metabolic rate, so that the body's daily caloric requirement may be little more than 1,000 calories. Some dieters cannot lose on a diet of more than 500 calories per day.*

*I do not think your diet is dangerous, but I would not advise taking in much less than 1,000 calories or you may not get enough protein, iron, and essential vitamins and minerals.*

David L. Smith, M.D.

Moderate cycling (12 to 15 miles per hour) for one hour is said to require about 300 calories. Yet to maintain this speed on level ground and no wind requires only 0.10 horsepower which converts to 64 calories per hour. Since the average sedentary man burns up 100 calories per hour, it would appear that the cyclist is apt to get fat rather than fit. Obviously, there is a difference between work output and food energy input. To get 64 kilocalories of work apparently requires about 300 calories of food. Can one always assume that the conversion efficiency of the average man is only 21 percent or does this vary with work output? For example, pedaling at 20 miles per hour requires an output of 130 calories per hour. Can I assume that the input is about five times this?

S. T. B., Indianapolis, IN

*Your question is well put and covers an area that is often misunderstood. Like other internal-combustion engines, when fuel (food) is oxidized, the body converts the released energy into heat and mechanical work. The efficiency of an engine is calculated as the percentage of energy that is converted into work instead of heat and, like most engines, the body's efficiency is in the range of 20 to 25 percent.*

*As you write, a sedentary, 70-kilogram man burns about 100 kilocalories per hour to maintain vital functions. When he applies 0.1 horsepower, or 64 kilocalories, to the road to maintain his bicycle speed for one hour, he is no longer sedentary. Heart, lungs, muscles, everything works harder, increasing metabolic and frictional heat which must be dissipated by the now-working sweat glands.*

*You are right. Four or five times more kilocalories are needed on the dinner plate than are required to propel the drive shaft. Fewer kilocalories are needed by the well-trained rider because he or she uses muscles more efficiently, but usually compensates by riding faster.*

*Cyclists get fat rather than fit when their food consumption covers conversation miles instead of actual road miles.*

Eugene A. Gaston, M.D.

I am 41 and because of my work and commuting time/distance am able to cycle usually only once each week. These weekend jaunts average 20 to 40 miles at 70 to 75 revolutions per minute in a 82.5-inch gear. I'm in excellent health, am 6 feet at 170 pounds, and easily pass the treadmill and all other tests in my doctor's office once annually. I am an office worker, and except for brisk daily walks and some intentional between-floor stair-climbing have no regular exercise program.

On these rides, which I continue throughout the summer here in Arizona's desert, I carry and consume one bottle of Body Punch and usually stop at a convenience market for a soft drink. Following the rides, I frequently get painful headaches through the temples and behind the eyes. Generally, I get more relief from Alka-Seltzer than from aspirin. My rides are always preceded by a hearty breakfast. I intend to continue cycling regardless, but do you have any recommendations for preventing or easing my headaches?

D. A., Woods, AZ

*Most of the rehydration drinks contain too much salt per ounce. I suspect you're suffering from a bit of dehydration coupled with electrolyte imbalance. As you know, the summer Arizona desert is quite capable of drawing large amounts of fluid from the body. Try weighing yourself before and after a ride to see how much fluid you are losing. (The amount of weight loss from burning foodstuffs is negligible.) I'd suggest increasing your fluid intake during your rides, mostly with water, until you have a loss of less than two pounds. A bit of extra potassium, such as using light salt on your food, may also help. I'd also suggest trying to find a way to get in some exercise during the week, even if it's only for half an hour on two nonconsecutive days.*

David L. Smith, M.D.

While cycling I would prefer to hydrate my body with an electrolyte solution rather than plain water. Gatorade can become expensive and is at times inaccessible. Can an equally effective and tasty solution be prepared at home from fruit juices? If so, what and how much would I add to the juice? Also, what percentage of total fluid intake can be of an electrolyte solution and not interfere with the body's normal electrolyte balance? My cycling consists of 15 to 30 minutes at a moderately brisk pace in 80° to 85°F. summer weather. I am a 25-year-old female with no history of heart disease, circulatory problems, or hypertension.

K. L. S., Corvallis, OR

*For a ride of only 15 to 30 minutes a day, elaborate preparation seems unnecessary. The American diet contains enough potassium for most people and probably too much sodium. I'd suggest riding for longer periods of time if you can: you won't get much aerobic benefit from only 15 minutes.*

*I'd suggest taking two water bottles, one with plain water and another with a somewhat diluted fruit juice or whatever you like to drink (stay away from carbonated beverages). Drink mostly the water, using the fruit juice for a change of pace.*

David L. Smith, M.D.

What food and drink should be taken on a five-to-six-hour, summertime cross-country ride?

A. C. P., Silver Spring, MD

*During a hot summer, a high water intake is essential. I'd suggest carrying two water bottles—a regular-size one that is easy to get at, and a full-quart size (which is very hard to get at). Most of your fluid intake should be plain water, but you can vary this with some electrolyte solution (such as ERG or Gatorade), lemonade, or orange juice. Carbonated drinks often cause cramps while riding.*

*Don't eat a lot before or during a ride; take in most of your food at the end of the day.*

David L. Smith, M.D.

# Part Three
# Pedaling
# and Conditioning

# Physiology of Pedaling: Leg Muscles

## David L. Smith, M.D.

The human body doesn't seem to have been designed with the bicycle in mind, but because of its marvelous complexity, the body is able to adapt to the rotary action of the cranks. There are three basic body systems at work when you are pedaling down the road: (1) the muscles themselves; (2) the cardiovascular system (heart, lungs, blood vessels); and (3) the nervous system which controls the actions of numbers 1 and 2.

There are basically three separate muscular actions during the downstroke of pedaling: extension of the thigh at the hip joint, extension of the leg at the knee joint, and extension of the foot at the ankle joint (if the "ankling" technique is used). Any aberration in pedaling technique that interferes with any of these actions will greatly reduce the number of muscles available to do the job, or force them to do their job in an inefficient manner. For example, the novice who tries to pedal his or her bike with the seat too low and heels on the pedals places all the load on the hip extensors by preventing knee and ankle extension.

The muscles that extend the lower limb in bicycling are the same ones that hold up our weight in walking and running; so they are much stronger than the muscles that flex the leg on the upstroke, and they don't have to work against body weight. A basic principle of body mechanics is that muscles operate to move the joint that they cross. A muscle attached to the pelvis and thighbone (femur) will operate the hip joint. A muscle attached to the pelvis and the lower leg will act on either the thigh or the lower leg or both, depending on what other muscles in the area are doing. For this reason, in bicycling, coordination is more important to efficiently get down the road than is brute force.

Without coordination of muscle pull, the leg muscles could all act against each other and wind up with no net force in any direction. There are many different leg muscles, large and small. The smaller ones, which I will not describe, are used for helping the large ones; for pulling the legs in directions not of concern to bicycling; and for fine control of leg, foot, and toe movement. I will describe the large muscles which deliver the power.

There are two major muscles in charge of extending the thigh: the gluteus maximus (the buttock muscle) and the adductor magnus. The gluteus maximus is attached to the back of the pelvis near the tailbone, wraps down over the ischial tubercle (perch bone), and attaches to the topside of the femur and to a thick tendonlike structure called the iliotibial band which eventually connects to the main lower leg bone (tibia). When it contracts, the thigh tends to extend (straighten) and rotate outward. The adductor magnus is connected to the front of the pelvic bone and extends down to the inside of the lower thighbone. It pulls the thigh in and extends it. Improper positioning of the legs—e.g., pedaling with your knees sticking out—will prevent this powerful muscle from doing its job.

The big set of muscles in the front and outside of the thigh, collectively known as the quadriceps femoris, delivers most of the knee extension (straightening) and also flexes the hip on the upstroke. They are connected to the pelvis and upper thighbone at the top and to the kneecap (patella) at the bottom. The kneecap is in turn connected to the larger lower leg bone (tibia).

The question of how high to put the seat is mostly a question of allowing the quadriceps femoris to operate in its most efficient range. For maximum efficiency, the knee should have a slight bend at the lowest pedal position. This muscle is also important in determining crank length. If you lengthen the cranks, you'll quickly reach a point of diminishing returns because the muscle becomes less efficient at the top of the stroke when the knee is flexed past 90 degrees. As the crank becomes longer, the flexion at the top of the stroke becomes greater and greater. Little or no efficiency is gained.

Bicyclists tend to think of ankling as a difficult trick achieved only after long practice. Actually, if the seat is at the proper height and toe clips are used to fix the foot in the proper position with the ball of the foot over the pedal spindle, the posterior leg muscles will be automatically brought into play to extend the ankle as the pedal approaches the bottom of the stroke. The main leg muscle, which you can easily feel when you stand on your toes, is called the gastrocnemius ("gastroc"). It is connected to the femur at the top and thus is capable of flexing the knee as well as extending the ankle. The muscle underneath it, called the soleus, is connected to the lower leg bones at the top. Both the gastroc and the soleus connect to the heel by the Achilles tendon.

Theoretically, the toe flexors could be used to further increase the pushing force. The body calls them into play more or less automatically to brace the foot during the downstroke, but I don't know of anybody who pedals with the toes. The to : extensors in the front of the leg are used in the clips to pull the ‿edal up during upstroke and are responsible for shin splints.

The professional spends a great deal of time strengthening the muscles that lift the leg so that he or she can pull the pedals around for a full 360-degree stroke with each leg. This is probably beyond most of us duffers, but almost anybody should be able to develop his or her lifting power until one leg does not have to use part of its strength to lift the other leg up.

# Physiology of Pedaling: Nervous System Control

## David L. Smith, M.D.

The kid down the block who is just learning to ride a bike is quite a sight to behold. The leg action is jerky, and when the bike starts to lean to one side, the rider frantically overreacts and turns the wheel so far that the bike tips over the other way. Then he or she forgets to pedal and falls off. In a few weeks, though, that kid will be pedaling all over the place, literally without giving it a second thought. Why?

The part of the brain that seems to be responsible for conscious thought is the cerebral cortex located at the very top of the brain. Bundles of nerve fibers called tracts lead to the cortex from the body and supply it with sensations such as sight and sense of muscle position. Other tracts lead from the cortex down through the spinal cord in order to direct the muscles.

The cerebral cortex, however, is quite limited in the number of different things it can pay attention to at once. If the cortex is busy commanding the arms to turn the handlebars, it is likely to forget to make the legs pedal.

Behind and underneath the cortex is a smaller section of the brain, called the cerebellum. The cerebellum can be compared to an automatic pilot or on-board computer. After it has been programmed to perform an action, it can take over the details and do a much better job than the cortex can. It is chiefly responsible for what we call coordination and helps us perform many automatic actions such as walking or getting the food from plate to mouth. Without the cerebellum, muscle actions are jerky and inaccurate; with it, the cortex can "leave the driving to us" and enjoy the scenery.

The same section of the cerebral cortex that sends fibers down the spinal cord to the muscles also sends fibers to the cerebellum so that it can teach the cerebellum a new task, or override its action. The cerebellum, in turn, sends tracts down the spinal cord to perform its function on the muscles. The cerebellum can't talk back or try to take over because it doesn't have any tracts going back up to the cortex.

The hypothalamus is a section of the brain that is more independent of the cortex. It is located deep inside the brain, sitting on top of the base of the skull near the pituitary gland. It is responsible for many automatic functions such as heart rate, body temperature, and hormonal regulation. If the muscles of the legs are churning along using gobs of oxygen and putting out liters of carbon dioxide, the hypothalamus notes the change in oxygen and carbon dioxide dissolved in the blood and increases lung action to compensate. If the heat output of the muscles causes the deep body temperature to begin rising, the hypothalamus causes the blood vessels under the skin to dilate so that the heat can radiate out through the skin and cool the blood off. It also regulates sweat output and blood pressure to compensate for exercise. It's also involved in the basic sensations of pleasure and pain and emotions.

There are plenty of other sections of the brain involved in the seemingly simple act of pedaling down the road, but my knowledge of anatomy is too limited to enable me to tell you much about them. The cerebellum and hypothalamus are chiefly responsible for the fact that bicycling is a pleasurable activity that you can do without having to think about it very much.

# Physiology and Pedaling: The Cardiovascular System

### David L. Smith, M.D.

The muscles involved in spinning the chainwheel around, like any other motor, combine fuel with oxygen to produce energy and waste products. It is, of course, the job of the blood to supply the fuel and oxygen and to take away the wastes. Although the muscles can use other fuels in a pinch, the primary energy source for muscles is glucose, a simple sugar. Glucose is supplied either directly from the intestine when it is absorbed, or it can be produced in the liver by chemical conversion of fats or protein. Glucose is made of carbon, oxygen, and hydrogen and when burned completely, produces carbon dioxide and water.

The oxygen in the bloodstream is carried in a unique chemical combination with hemoglobin in the red blood cell. It is picked up by the red cell in the presence of a high ambient oxygen concentration, such as is found in the lungs. In an area where the overall oxygen concentration is low, such as in a working muscle, the red cell releases oxygen to the surrounding tissues. Oxygen can be held in the muscle cell temporarily by myoglobin (similar to hemoglobin) until it is used. Both hemoglobin and myoglobin contain iron atoms; if a person is iron deficient, a shortage of hemoglobin and myoglobin develops and the exercise capacity is decreased.

When a muscle is loafing, the demand for oxygen is minimal. The blood supply to that muscle is relatively small, and the red cells going back to the heart and lungs still have a lot of oxygen in them.

When a muscle is exercised, several things happen. The red cells have more oxygen taken from them as they go through the muscle, and go back to the heart and lungs in a relatively empty condition. The blood vessels going through the muscle dilate to allow a greater blood supply. The heart increases its output by increasing both rate and force of pumping. The lungs similarly work harder. These measures are sufficient to keep up with muscular demand in a long-term, moderate output situation such as a century ride.

In a sprint, however, the muscles quickly outstrip the oxygen supply available. In this situation, the muscles can switch temporarily to anaerobic metabolism, which means that they produce energy from glucose without using oxygen. This is an inefficient process and produces large amounts of waste products called pyruvic and lactic acids, which are responsible for much of the muscle discomfort produced in such a situation. After the sprint is won or lost, body cells take up and metabolize the anaerobic waste products, and the lungs huff and puff until the red cells are full of oxygen again.

A few years ago, my wife and I decided to tour the south rim of the Grand Canyon. We had a big breakfast and got rather a late start. It was already hot when we set out. Midway up the second hill my wife got off her bike and fainted right in the middle of the road. My medical reconstruction of that event is this: the blood vessels of her intestines were dilated which allowed a large amount of blood to flow through to pick up her breakfast and take it to the other body cells. Her skin capillaries were similarly dilated because of the heat to allow blood to flow through and cool the body cells off. When her muscle blood vessels dilated to bring in more oxygen, the body's demand for blood flow became more than her heart could supply, and she had a "brownout." With blood pressure too low to pump the blood up to her brain, she fainted.

This incident illustrates several principles of diet and exercise: (1) Keep your diet simple if you plan to race or tour after a meal. Emphasize sugars and starches, which require little digestion and provide quick energy. Avoid fats and protein, which take longer and are more difficult to digest. (2) If the weather is hot, limit your output to what your blood system can handle, or you may faint or have a heat stroke. (3) Training and conditioning increase your cardiovascular system's output capacity just as they increase your muscle output. Even if you are young and healthy, your cardiovascular system can be quite out of shape if you don't stress it regularly with exercise.

# Medical Q and A

I have recently read something in two different books which should interest beginning bicycle tourists. *Running Scared* by Tex Maule (New York: Saturday Review Press, 1972) is an autobiographical account of his recovery from a heart attack. After his attack he started jogging and gradually worked up to running more than 10 miles a day. He found there was a sort of threshold at about 3 miles; up to that point he and other joggers made progress slowly and with much effort, but beyond the threshold it was comparatively easy to increase both distance and speed.

Dr. Kenneth Cooper, in his book *Aerobics* (New York: Evans, 1968), gives examples of what seems to be the same thing. He states, "Men who begin conditioning programs agonize for months trying to get the oxygen where it's needed, then BOOM!, almost overnight the exercise becomes relatively effortless."

Is this threshold experience common among bicycle tourists? If so, where, for most people, is it?

J. W. W., San Francisco, CA

You pose an interesting question. I am well aware of the threshold experience, having gone through it some months after I started jogging. Bicycle racers probably have similar experiences, although I cannot recall that I did, probably because I did not train hard enough. Frank Whitt and David Wilson in Bicycling Science (Cambridge, MA: MIT Press, 1974), after comparing sprint runners with track racers, concluded that the power required for bicycling is about one-fifth that needed for running at the same speed. If the ratio between joggers and bicycle tourists is the same and joggers "threshold" at 3 miles, tourists should do the same at about 15 miles. In hundreds (maybe thousands) of conversations with bicycle tourists of all degrees of ability, I have never once heard the threshold experience mentioned.

Eugene A. Gaston, M.D.

Perhaps you can help me in solving something of a dilemma with respect to Dr. Kenneth Cooper's aerobics program as it relates to cycling. In his book, Dr. Cooper instructs that the point value for miles cycled should be reduced by ½ point per mile if a racing bicycle is used since his point values are based on the use of a standard 1-speed machine. The only other mention he makes of bicycles in the book is to designate a 3-speed as a racing bicycle. Nowhere does he mention the 10-speed.

I'm interested in determining what point value should be given to cycling using a 10-speed since I neither want to take advantage of a point system based on 1-speed gearing, nor do I want to penalize myself unnecessarily.

J. B. T., Wheaton, MD

Dr. Cooper is a runner, not a cyclist. In his testing to set up a point system, he apparently did not use an ergometer, nor did he use a self-contained telemetric apparatus such as the Japanese Bicycle Research Association has used. Here is Dr. Cooper's description of his tests (Aerobics, p. 47, Bantam edition, 1972): "We rigged a Rube Goldberg attachment to the back of a pickup truck, installed our EKG machine and expired-air collectors on it, then had the subject cycle behind the truck at various speeds and distances." In other words, this was a motor-paced test rather than a test of free-air cycling. Also, the type of bicycle was not specified in the book.

Dr. Cooper has since updated the point system for bicycling in several of his more recent books. According to the latest, The New Aerobics (New York: Bantam, 1970), "Experience has shown that the difference in energy expended on various types of bicycles is not great enough to require adjustment of the point chart. Since the chart is set up to allow a certain margin of error, you'll be getting the total point value from your exercise even if you ride a 10-speed racer." If you've been subtracting aerobic points because you read an earlier edition, cheer up. You have been doing even better than you thought!

David L. Smith, M.D.

A friend and I have been cycling quite extensively this past year. We both have noticed that when we stand up quickly after sitting for a while, we feel faint. We never faint when exerting ourselves while riding. Could this possibly be from having a lower resting blood pressure?

T. E., Santa Clara, CA

*Yes, this is partially due to a low resting blood pressure. It's also due to pooling of blood in the leg veins and shunting of blood away from the head to the skin for cooling purposes. While you're riding, the blood pressure rises, and blood in the leg veins is pumped back to the heart by the contractions of the leg muscles.*

*Your "postural hypotension" is really a sign of good health; I've not seen anyone with high blood pressure who ever had this problem.*

David L. Smith, M.D.

I am 55 and in general good health except for a moderate case of arthritis. During the last year and a half I have put about 2,600 miles on my bike. Last week I suffered a mild stroke called a T.I.A. (transient ischemic attack). Although now completely recovered, my doctor has me on five milligrams a day of an anticoagulant, Coumadin Sodium, for the next six months. Although I have full confidence in his advice about not riding my bike for the next six months, I was wondering if there might be some exercise program to help get that six months over with sooner.

M. J. F., Austin, TX

*I assume that your doctor told you not to ride your bike because he feared you might have another attack while out in the country alone. This is a legitimate concern.*

*You may have a bigger problem than you realize. It is a little unusual for a fellow your age to be having a T.I.A., and it suggests that you may have a considerable amount of arteriosclerosis (hardening of the arteries). If your doctor has not already done so, I would suggest a complete workup including stress testing with an*

67

EKG; and blood pressure, blood lipid, diabetes, and uric acid tests. Any abnormalities found, when corrected, will considerably lessen your chances of another cardiovascular event.

If you smoke, STOP. If the stress test shows evidence of clogging of the coronary arteries, then a very carefully supervised exercise program should be undertaken. Any excess weight must come off.

There are any number of activities that can offer the same exercise benefits to the heart as cycling. These include running, swimming, cross-country skiing, tennis, and handball. Pick the one that you and your doctor like the best.

David L. Smith, M.D.

I developed high blood pressure and am watching my salt intake and taking medication. When bicycling in hot weather, one perspires and loses a lot of salt, even though sodium intake must be kept low. What is there to do about this problem?

S. I., Brooklyn, NY

Your problem is not an insoluble dilemma. In hot weather the body does lose some salt in sweat, but water loss is proportionately much greater, especially in cyclists acclimated to exercising in hot weather. It is not necessary in most instances to take salt tablets to prevent heat exhaustion. I would recommend that when cycling in hot weather, you take the following precautions:

1. Keep an electrolyte solution, such as Gatorade, in your water bottle and partake liberally.
2. Dress as lightly as possible.
3. Take it easy. You aren't trying to win the Tour de France.
4. When it is really hot, keep your shirt wet from a water bottle. This will decrease the amount of sweating.

There is one other problem of concern, that of potassium loss. Vigorous exercise can promote loss of body potassium through the urine. Some medicines for high blood pressure also produce potassium loss. Your doctor can prescribe a potassium supplement for you or prescribe medicines that do not tend to produce potassium loss.

I encourage you to continue to bicycle. Physical fitness and loss of excess weight is generally quite beneficial in controlling high blood pressure.

David L. Smith, M.D.

# Part Four
# Choosing and Using Saddles

# Choosing a Saddle

## David L. Smith, M.D.

The saddle that came with my new bike certainly looked satisfactory. It was made out of real leather and looked like those narrow saddles the racers use. The only trouble was that after about 20 miles it felt like I was sitting on the bare seatpost. I thought the saddle just needed breaking in, but after a year and 2,500 miles, it still felt like a bare seatpost. I have now studied the portions of my anatomy involved, and, armed with this knowledge, have found a comfortable saddle.

The first thing you must know before saddle-shopping, is your interischiadic distance. This rather personal measurement is the distance between your ischial tuberositates, or sit bones. They can be felt underneath the buttock muscles, just north of the rectum. The width of a saddle must be one to two inches wider than this distance for comfort, so that body weight is borne by the sit bones rather than by the sensitive tissues between the sit bones. This distance is usually greater for the female pelvis.

In general, the better-grade leather touring saddles put out by Brooks and Ideale have adequate width for the males. The Brooks B72 is the only good saddle I know of that has adequate width (8½ inches) for most women.

There are several other tricks to buying and using an adequate saddle. Here are all the ones I know of:

**Material:** High-grade leather (expensive leather) has the right amount of resiliency to produce just the right amount of give while supporting body weight. This is not to say that nylon and plastic can't be comfortable, but your chances of buying a comfortable saddle the first time around are a lot greater if you buy leather.

**Shape:** A good saddle is teardrop shaped when viewed from the top, rather than round or wedge shaped. It narrows sharply to allow room for the thighs to work without chafing. The nose is long enough and wide enough to spread weight over the entire crotch.

**Position:** Most cyclists prefer a neutral or slightly nose-up position. The nose should tilt upward far enough to keep the sit bones on the wide part of the saddle but not so far that pain or numbness of the crotch is produced.

**Springs:** Springs of any sort waste energy and are an anathema to most serious cyclists. However, they are useful in a few situations. They greatly increase comfort for people who prefer an upright riding style. They reduce road shock for the rear rider on a tandem, who is placed at a disadvantage at seeing and avoiding the bumps. The saddle with springs which I recommend is the Brooks B66 for the ladies. It is good for people with bad backs, especially with a history of disk problems.

**Breaking-in:** Some people beat their bad saddles with rolling pins and other blunt instruments. Others try positive-reinforcement techniques such as rubbing them with neat's-foot oil. If either of these methods helps, by all means do it. An expensive saddle, if suited for you in the first place, will get more comfortable with age. I'm not sure, though, if it is the saddle that is breaking in, or the rider. Cheap saddles only get more uncomfortable.

**Saddle Care:** Leather saddles should be washed occasionally with saddle soap and then given a coat of clear (neutral) shoe polish. (Shoe polish with dye will rub off on your pants.) They should be protected from the rain, such as by a shower cap. With minimum care, a good saddle can last for many years.

# Medical Q and A

I am 44 years old, in pretty good shape, 6 feet tall, and 185 pounds. I have been involved in bicycling for a number of years and about three years ago found that biking was my best outlet for exercise and commuting. I began to consider a cross-country tour and last summer I made plans, looking into such things as equipment. Last winter I started working out on rollers and would do about an hour's riding on an average of 6 days a week. When the snow was off the roads, I went back to my routine of riding to work and did this on an average of 9 out of 10 days this spring.

My problem is, on the first day out after an easy 40 miles, I noticed what I will call a *numb crotch*. To be more specific, my genital region became almost lacking in feeling. I rested long and easy that first night but found that in the morning the feeling had not returned. I continued my trip in easy stages for 10 days, covering about 650 miles, but became so concerned over the increasing numbness that I decided it would be best to stop.

I have been home for 10 days now and find that by doing no biking the feeling is starting to come back. I was using an Ideale 90 saddle (the pretreated one), had it adjusted to a comfortable position, and had put perhaps 600 miles on it before the start of the trip. I had only a bit of saddle soreness the first few days, but no problems other than the numb crotch.

I have asked some of the bike-shop people in the area, but all I get are a few chuckles and no answers, as no one else seems to have had this problem. I would like very much to keep on biking and would like to be able to tour. How am I going to solve this problem?

G. L. B., Cape Elizabeth, ME

*I am surprised that this complaint is not more common. Perhaps embarrassment prevents many sufferers from mentioning it.*

*Sensation is carried from the penis (or clitoris) and perineum to the brain by the pudendal nerves, one on each side. The numbness was caused by injury to these nerves when they were compressed between the saddle and the pelvic bones. The same type of injury causes numbness of the hands when nerves are compressed between wrist bones and the handlebars. The nerves will recover in a few weeks or months after the injury, and you should stay off the bike until sensation has returned to normal.*

*To prevent recurrence, a different saddle may be necessary, but first try changing the angle of your present saddle. My guess is that lowering the front end a few degrees will solve the problem. If it does not, try raising the handlebars and/or shortening the distance between saddle and handlebars.*

Eugene A. Gaston, M.D.

My age is 55; I'm 5 feet, 9 inches; 173 pounds; and in excellent health. However, I developed a dull pain in the coccyx or pubic area. I thought the symptom might be "coachman's bottom," where the bursae over the ischial tubercles become inflamed. Not so. In my case, the pain is in an area too high. I submitted to a proctoscope examination, and the results were okay.

I certainly enjoy the sport but am wondering if this is chronic and means the demise of my bike riding? What would you recommend?

M. T., Westerville, OH

*The coccyx, or tailbone, is said to be left over from the time when our ancestors were swinging through trees and is about as useful as the appendix. Repeated low-grade trauma often leads to soreness, especially in those of us who are middle-aged. Arthritis can even develop in the joint between the coccyx and the sacrum, and I think this is what you may have. The doctor can treat this by removing the coccyx surgically, or perhaps ease the pain by some steroid injections to the joint area. However, you can probably relieve a lot of the discomfort by employing various measures to get your weight off the structures in the midline. This includes using a saddle that is wide enough (at least one inch wider than the distance between the ischial tubercles) to put your weight on these structures. It may also help to modify your sitting position to put more weight on your arms.*

*I have also used a sheepskin pad but have found that a wider saddle did a better job of solving my discomfort and does not chafe my legs.*

David L. Smith, M.D.

# Part Five
# Bikers' Knees

# Problems and Solutions

## Eugene A. Gaston, M.D.

The most frequent knee problems of bicyclists are chondromalacia, strains, and sprains. Fractures of bones and/or cartilages are more common to other sports. The rider with some knowledge of the anatomy and physiology of the knees may be able to prevent these injuries or treat them properly before they become chronic and disabling. The following is presented with that in mind.

It is essential that the reader understand certain basic descriptive terms. Directions are described as: anterior, toward the front of the body; posterior, toward the back; medial, toward the midline of the body; lateral, away from midline; cephalad, toward the head; caudad, toward the feet; distal, away from the point of origin; proximal, toward the point of origin. Joint motions are described as: flexion, bending; extension, straightening; abduction, away from the midline of the body; adduction, toward the midline.

Three bones are involved in the knee joint: the femur or thighbone; the tibia, the larger of the two bones of the lower leg; and the patella or kneecap. The fibula, the smaller bone of the leg, is not part of the joint. The distal end of the femur is divided into two more-or-less hemispherical knobs, called condyles, which are separated by a deep groove, the anterior part of which acts as a guide for the patella. The caudad portion of the groove acts as a guide for a bony ridge on the cephalad surface of the tibia. The ridge, riding in the groove, prevents the two bones from sliding medially or laterally in relation to each other.

The cephalad surface of the tibia is divided into two relatively flat areas called plateaus, which are separated by the bony ridge mentioned above. The plateaus are converted into shallow sockets for the femoral condyles by crescent-shaped cartilages, about ½-inch wide, which are loosely adherent to the periphery of the plateaus and are thicker on the outside than toward the centers. These cartilages are frequently fractured in contact sports, necessitating the well-publicized knee surgery of professional athletes.

The tendon that connects the quadriceps muscle on the front of the thigh to the tibial tubercle on the front of the tibia below the knee has two names that are used interchangeably: quadriceps tendon and patellar tendon. The patella develops within the substance of this tendon, a thin portion of the tendon covering its anterior surface and the remainder of the tendon being attached around its periphery. The posterior surface of the patella and all of the joint surfaces of the femur and tibia are covered with cartilage, which has a smooth surface that reduces friction. By sliding up and down in the groove between the condyles during extension and flexion of the knee, the patella aligns the tendon so it always pulls in exactly the same direction. The patella also increases the leverage of the quadriceps by making it pull on the tibia at a greater angle. Without the patella, the quadriceps would need to be 30 percent stronger to produce the force that is largely, but not completely, responsible for pushing the pedals.

Normal muscles can exert a force of about 42 pounds per square inch of cross-sectional area; and the quadriceps, one of the largest muscles in the body, can exert a maximum of about 700 pounds. A not insignificant force is thus applied directly to the cartilage-covered surfaces of the patella and femoral condyles as they slide, one upon the other, with each rotation of the crank. It seems probable that chondromalacia, a degeneration of knee cartilages that starts on the posterior surface of the patella, is somehow related to the magnitude of this stress. Low gears reduce the force necessary to turn the cranks and may be important in eliminating the initial injury. They are certainly important in preventing aggravation of the condition once it starts.

The knee, like other joints or any mechanical linkage, requires lubrication. This is supplied by synovia, a clear viscous fluid that is secreted by a membrane (called the synovial membrane) which lines all joints. When irritated by injury or disease, the membrane secretes excessive amounts of fluid, and swelling of the joint results. If there is a sufficient excess of fluid in the knee, the swelling extends cephalad because the suprapatellar bursa, a sac that lies by the quadriceps and anterior to the distal femur, becomes distended. Aspiration of excess fluid, with or without injections of cortisone, is useful for the treatment of some joint conditions.

Stability of the knee depends largely on the ligaments, which hold the bones together, and the muscles, which activate the joint. The bones are so shaped that they contribute relatively little to joint stability. The joint capsule, which encloses the knee, is made of strong, ligamentous tissue and is reinforced on the medial and lateral sides by the very strong collateral ligaments, which prevent abduction or adduction. Within the knee are two short cruciate ligaments that prevent the tibia from moving anteriorly or posteriorly in relation to the femur. The knee is protected anteriorly by the patella and the quadriceps tendon and is protected posteriorly by the hamstrings and other muscles responsible for flexion.

Injuries to knee ligaments are common to bicyclists. The terms strain and sprain describe these injuries, both indicating that some of the cells making up the ligament have been torn or damaged. Strain indicates less injury than sprain. The patellar ligament and the collateral ligaments, on the medial and lateral sides of the knee, are frequently injured; the former by stresses resulting from pushing too hard in high gears, and the latter by similar but differently placed stresses often caused by improper placement of the feet on the pedals. When the patellar ligament is injured, pain and tenderness occur on the anterior surface and around the periphery of the patella. How to prevent and treat this injury is obvious: use lower gears.

Medial (counterclockwise) rotation of the tibia occurs normally when the knee is flexed and external rotation when it is extended. These rotations are so slight that the flexibility of the ankle and foot joints makes shifting positions of the feet on the pedals unnecessary. When the feet are placed on the pedals with the toes pointing too far laterally, however, force of sufficient magnitude to sometimes cause injury is applied to the medial collateral ligaments. The resulting strain or sprain causes pain and tenderness medial to the patella. Similarly, if the toes point too far medially (pigeon-toes), injury to the lateral collateral ligaments can result, with pain and tenderness lateral to the patella. The use of proper gears, the position of the feet on the pedals, and the angulation of shoe cleats are thus important to prevent these minor but disabling injuries.

Bicyclists who have knock-knees or bowlegs put additional stresses on the collateral ligaments, and even slight degrees of these anatomical variations cause ligamentous injury. Changes of the angles through which the soles of the feet press on the pedals will often relieve the pain of such injuries. Riders with knock-knees may relieve strain of the medial collateral ligaments by building up the medial side of pedals (or shoes) so the angle of pressure is changed by a few degrees. Similarly, those with bowlegs may obtain relief by building up the lateral sides.

# Medical Q and A

I am 31 years old, and after years of off-and-on cycling, I began riding 10 miles during the week and up to 50 miles per day on weekends. Following what turned out to be a climactic 50-mile ride, I developed pain in my left knee, which doctors at a sports medicine clinic diagnosed as inflammation under the patella. They prescribed no cycling until the pain subsided and exercises which included straight leg lifts with weights on the ankles. I did not follow up on the exercises, and after several months away from cycling, a few miles on the bike or even hiking on hilly terrain causes a grating sensation in my knees, if not the outright pain I had before.

Are my bicycling days over? Have I done irreparable damage by my enthusiastic riding? Shall I sell my fine lightweight bicycle which has given me so many hours of unparalleled enjoyment?

R. P. G., Port Townsend, WA

*The clinic doctors used the word inflammation to describe a degeneration of the knee cartilages called chondromalacia. This starts on the undersurface of the patella and may progress to involve all of the cartilaginous joint surfaces, with severe and permanent crippling. In advanced stages, even surgery is far from satisfactory. This is the reason doctors took your symptoms so seriously and advised you to stop bicycling.*

*While the ultimate cause of chondromalacia is not known, it is definitely related to exertion. When the initiating injury is stopped in the early stages of the disease, recovery is usually complete. The straight-leg-raising exercises were prescribed to prevent atrophy and weakening of the quadriceps muscles, which occurs very soon after mobility of the knees is diminished even slightly. Weakening of the quadriceps lessens the stability of the joint and prolongs recovery.*

*The pain having been replaced by a grating sensation suggests that you are improving. Follow the good advice you have been given, including the quadriceps exercises. Don't sell your bike.*

Eugene A. Gaston, M.D.

Fifteen years ago I first noticed a slight numb pain in both knees when walking downhill or stepping off curbs. I eventually concluded that this was caused by deep knee bends while doing weight lifting exercises in a cold shed. A specialist told me there was nothing wrong with my knees, and six months later an army doctor told me I had a "common problem," wrapped up my knees and sent me back to duty.

At the start of cool weather in the fall of 1975, after I had become a serious bicyclist, the knee trouble first became bad enough to be described as pain. A month earlier in warm weather I was able to ride 100 miles but was now coasting back in pain after only 15 miles. During the past two winters I have found a good set of elastic bands that stay in place and seem to be the cure. They even help a great deal in summer. I still walk up most hills, but all I really want is endurance. Will my present activities degrade my knees any farther? Should I see a specialist?

R. G., Warwick, RI

*The cold temperature of the training shed could not penetrate into the knee joints (the rapid circulation of warm blood takes care of that) and has nothing to do with your problem. Deep knee bends, however, have been dropped from most training programs because of their deleterious effects on knee cartilages, and this is almost certainly when your trouble started. Your present symptoms are characteristic of chondromalacia. The elastic knee supports will not effect a cure. I strongly advise you to see a specialist.*

Eugene A. Gaston, M.D.

I am a 22-year-old man with proportionately strong legs. Last summer, midway through a six-week tour, pain developed in my left knee. It was directly under the kneecap, would start after about 5 miles, and begin to let up after about 20 miles. I had no trouble during the winter when I did not ride, but on the first significant bike trip this spring the stiffness and pain returned. My doctor found nothing wrong. Could the pain be caused by my equipment? Would cranks of different length, shorter toe clips (I wear size-6 shoes), or changing the height of the saddle help?

G. S., Bronx, NY

*Your mention of strong legs implies that you like to push hard in high gears rather than spin in lower gears. The location of the pain suggests early chondromalacia, possibly the result of too much pressure on the patella from the use of high gears. If you are a pusher, change your habits and use lower gears.*

*Have your entire bicycle, including the cranks, toe clips, and saddle, adjusted to your build. The best discussion of this that I have* seen starts on page 61 of DeLong's Guide to Bicycles and Bicycling: The Art and Science by Fred DeLong (Radnor, PA: Chilton, 1974).

In addition, the angle of the foot on the pedal, whether toed in or out, and the pressure angle should be varied until relief is obtained. If the pain continues, see your doctor again.

Eugene A. Gaston, M.D.

# Part Six
# The Cycling
# Environment

# Medical Q and A

Are there any dangers involved in breathing very cold air into the lungs, especially under physical stress due to vigorous exercise?

M. B., Northbrook, IL

*I know of no instances of lung damage due to breathing unpolluted cold air. Experts tell me that by the time the air gets to the lungs, it has been fully humidified and brought to body temperature. It is preferable to breathe through the nose rather than the mouth, as the nose does a better job of this.*

David L. Smith, M.D.

I am 56 years old and have been a bicycle commuter most of my life. During the past five years I have used a suburban route of about 12 miles, with variations chosen to avoid traffic and pollution as much as possible, though some of the route is along heavily traveled roads. I am as strong as ever and feel fine, but one year ago the Red Cross rejected me as a donor because I have iron-deficiency anemia. In past years I have donated more than 11 gallons of blood but have given none during the past year, yet my blood has not returned to normal. After many tests my doctor has found no source of blood loss and no medical problem except a low iron level. A connection with cycling suggests itself because a good friend, also a long-term bicycle commuter, has developed the same problem. What are the possible long-term effects of low-level pollution such as we may be experiencing? Is anemia a possible result?

G.M.K., Ph.D., Oxon Hill, MD

*Exercise, including bicycling, does not cause anemia. At one time marathon runners were believed to develop anemia because the trauma of the feet hitting the pavement injures a certain number of blood cells with each step. Bicyclists do not, of course, suffer this* kind of trauma, and recent studies of runners in the Boston Marathon have failed to demonstrate the anemia. The amount of air pollution to which you are exposed is not significant from a health standpoint and is not the cause of the anemia. Rather, it's probably the 11-plus gallons of blood you have so generously donated. Medicine containing iron has probably been prescribed by your doctor, and the deficiency will eventually be corrected.

Eugene A. Gaston, M.D.

For days on end last summer the air quality in the Baltimore area was described by the Maryland State Department of Health as "hazardous." This translates to ozone levels ranging from 0.1 to 0.249 ppm, often hovering at about 0.2 ppm. During these times the local media advised the elderly, infants, and people with chest problems to stay indoors and take it easy.

What does this level of air pollution mean for bike riders, joggers, and others who exercise vigorously and are in top physical shape? Should we take precautions too?

H. M. H., Baltimore, MD

Ozone levels indicate the concentration of a number of highly toxic pollutants, called oxidants, which result from the sun's radiant energy acting on hydrocarbons and oxides of nitrogen. Collectively these are called photochemical smog. Because sunshine is necessary for their formation, peak levels occur at midday, and high levels accumulate when the air is stagnant due to temperature inversions. Automobile and industrial exhausts supply the hydrocarbons, thus the central city at high noon on a muggy day with no wind is the worst place for strenuous exercise. The less congested suburbs and the central city in early morning and evening are safe, except under very unusual circumstances.

Years of repeated exposure to polluted air are necessary to permanently injure healthy lungs. Smoking cigarettes is much more dangerous than the pollution you describe.

Eugene A. Gaston, M.D.

Do you have any special recommendations for winter riding?

C. E., Nashville, TN

With care, you should be able to ride every day this winter except when there is too much snow or ice on the road, or when it is both too cold and too wet (raining or snowing).

I'd suggest the following guidelines for riding and clothing:

Stay dry and out of rain and snow; do not overdress or you will *sweat and then start chilling. Stay slightly on the cool side all the time.*

*Feet, hands, ears and noses require the most care. Give them as much protection as you can. In winter I use a motorcycle helmet that covers my ears, a ski mask, lined gloves, double socks and un-ventilated shoes, plus waterproof shoe covers if the ground is wet.*

*Wool is still the best protector against cold; in extreme cold fiberfill garments are good. Down garments are good if they are kept dry, but they are very expensive. Gore-Tex is advertised as being the best material for wet-weather riding but is also very expensive. Coated nylon is cheaper.*

*Wear several thin layers of clothes rather than one thick layer so that you can take layers off as you warm up.*

*The chest may need more layers than the back because of wind chill factor. Newspapers are good for this.*

*Take off layers at the bottom of a climb; put them back on at the top.*

*I don't know of any particular temperature or wind chill factor that precludes biking if adequate precautions are taken.*

David L. Smith, M.D.

I am a 25-year-old cyclist/runner who finds himself crippled and unable to cycle or run when the weather gets below about 55°F. In reasonable shape, I've made cross-country tours and enjoy both types of exercise all summer long. But when autumn sets in, a strange tightness in my upper trachea occurs along with coughing, wheezing, and inability to get a good deep breath when I run at a reasonable rate or when I cycle. It seems to be some sort of allergy, and I have consulted my doctor about it. There is no lung damage; I do not smoke; and I'm not overweight. Right now I take about one-fourth of an Actifed when it comes on. Is it possible to be allergic to cool/cold weather? It takes all the fun out of exercising when I have to fight for air or run on Actifeds. I'm tired of getting fat all winter. Any suggestions?

R. S., Indianapolis, IN

*You have asthma, or spasm of the bronchial tubes, and in your case, allergy to cold is the most important of two causes. Exercise is also a cause, and pulmonary function tests done while running on a treadmill or riding a bicycle ergometer would determine its part in precipitating attacks. Information from such tests might help with treatment.*

*Actifed, an antihistamine, controls your symptoms and can be continued without risk. Cromolyn sodium, a powder that is inhaled with the aid of a rubber bulb blower, effectively prevents attacks but is of no value after the wheezing starts. Using it before exercise might be a more effective way of controlling symptoms.*

Eugene A. Gaston, M.D.

I have been reading about riding in cold weather and keeping the knees warm. I ride to work, which is about 11 miles one way, with a lot of hills. I ride all year, even in temperatures below zero. I would like to have your opinion on these problems.

When the temperature is 40°F. or above I usually ride in shorts. My knees don't feel cold, but my legs will feel cold to the touch. How warm should I keep my knees?

I have been told that breathing in very cold air will damage the lungs. I used to cover my mouth with a muffler in the cold (10°F. or below), but lately I have been experimenting by leaving my mouth open. It does not seem to bother me except for the first mile or so.

I ride about six minutes before my first big hill. Is this enough warm-up time? I try to do all my riding in gears that allow me to pump without straining or spinning too fast.

L. F., Lecompton, KS

*If you are comfortable, don't worry. You should increase your knee covering if your knees are cold or if you develop any painful knee problems.*

*In cold weather breathe through your nose as much as possible. It does a better job of warming and humidifying the air. I have seen nothing in medical journals about "frozen lungs" south of the Arctic Circle, but a muffler or other mouth covering should at least improve comfort.*

*Exercise physiologists recommend about 10 minutes of warming up before heavy exercise. I should think 6 minutes would be enough if you are comfortable.*

David L. Smith, M.D.

I would appreciate your comments on cycling at high altitudes. I plan on cycling at peak altitudes of approximately 12,000 feet; while I plan to be in top condition, I am uncertain as to how much acclimatization time I can or should allow. Most of my conditioning is aerobic or mildly anaerobic. Is heavy anaerobic activity such as wind sprinting and interval training required? My present training is done below 1,000 feet.

F. B. P., M.D., Des Moines, IA

*If any significant numbers of flatland tourists try to climb to 12,000 feet without acclimatization, there is certainly the possibility of somebody getting altitude sickness.*

*There are really two problems here: performance at altitude and mountain sickness. Even with acclimatization, performance will be decreased almost 20 percent at 12,000 feet. (A decrease of approximately 3 to 3½ percent for each 1,000 feet of elevation above 5,000 feet is to be expected.) There isn't much you can do about this except to be in as good shape aerobically as possible and fit your bike with lower gears. Anaerobic training is very helpful for hill climbs, but I don't think it will specifically help altitude performance. For more about this read pages 350–61 in* The Physiological Basis of Physical Education and Athletics *(Mathews, D. and Fox, E. 2d ed. Philadelphia: Saunders, 1976).*

*To prevent mountain sickness and for optimal performance, you should acclimatize for two to three weeks before maximal exertion at 10,000 to 12,000 feet. If you're unable to take this much time, I'd suggest taking acetazolamide prophylactically. Acetazolamide has been helpful for mild altitude symptoms, but for severe mountain sickness there is no substitute for oxygen and removal to a lower altitude.*

David L. Smith, M.D.


I recently rode my bike on a century through the Livermore Valley. The temperatures became very high, but the first 50 miles went smoothly. Almost immediately following this midpoint, however, I started feeling mildly dizzy, nauseated, and very fatigued. Water did not seem to alleviate this condition at all. At the 60-mile point I got a can of soda, of which I could only drink about half. After 20 minutes, my condition improved slightly, and I was able to continue for another 20 miles at which point, I stopped for another half-can of soda. I noticed also that whenever I took a deep breath, my lungs hurt a bit, and I coughed slightly. I did not fully recover from the lung problem until about a day and a half later. I finally finished the century, but upon weighing myself afterward, found that I had lost 10 pounds.

My major problem seemed to be nutritional in nature, and I have become very interested in trying to find information about what the body needs when it is under prolonged physical stress. I would be very appreciative if you could direct me to some of the research in the area of endurance. I am very interested in trying to determine with some degree of accuracy if a nutritional balance can be maintained on long trips.

F. R., Mountain View, CA

I do not think your problem is nutritional. I think you were suffering from heat exhaustion due to excess losses of water and electrolytes, coupled with the very high temperature. Next summer, do the following:

Think twice about riding a full century if the temperature and humidity are both high.

Carry lots of fluids. A dilute electrolyte mix such as a mix of 2 parts water to 1 part Gatorade, although not very palatable, is good physiologically. I can carry up to 2 quarts on my bike using the largest available water bottles and all available places to mount them.

Drink lots as you ride (don't wait until a rest stop); try a pint of fluid every hour.

Take a five-minute break every one to two hours with more fluid ingestion.

If you lose more than five pounds after a ride, you didn't drink enough.

David L. Smith, M.D.

# Part Seven
# Compatible Sports

# Winter Sports Alternatives

## David L. Smith, M.D.

Wintertime in northern climes brings special problems for the cyclist. Cycling becomes less and less of a viable option as daylight hours shorten, roads become snow- or ice-covered, and temperatures drop to frostbite levels. Many a bicycle is hung up for months at a time, while thigh muscles shrink and waistlines expand. In the spring, much lost ground must be recovered at the cost of weeks or months of training.

There are, of course, many sports and exercises available during the winter. For the average nonathlete, as well as for many athletes, the value of any exercise must be weighed by its value in producing or maintaining aerobic fitness; that is, its ability to produce increases in long-term oxygen uptake or horsepower output. Aerobic fitness is felt to be beneficial in preventing heart attacks and several other disorders, and the cyclist who is fit will be able to pedal farther and more easily than the one who is not fit.

The American College of Sports Medicine is very interested in promoting cardiovascular fitness among the population. They make the following recommendations "for the quantity and quality of training for developing and maintaining cardiorespiratory fitness and body composition (fatness vs. leanness) in the healthy adult:

1. Frequency of training—three to five days per week;
2. Intensity of training—60 to 90 percent of maximum heart rate reserve, or 50 to 85 percent of maximum oxygen uptake;
3. Duration of training—15 to 60 minutes of continuous aerobic activity."

They further state that any activity that uses large muscle

groups, that can be maintained continuously and is rhythmical and aerobic in nature, is suitable. They cite as examples bicycling, running, walking–hiking, swimming, skating, cross-country skiiing, rope-skipping and various "endurance game" activities.

Obviously, some exercises and sports are more strenuous than others even among this list of rather strenuous activities. Also, the person doing the exercising has a choice of how hard he/she is going to work. For an equal amount of benefit, an exercise of lower intensity should be carried out for a longer period of time than an exercise of higher intensity. Because exercises of high intensity, such as hard running, are associated with more injuries and have more dropouts, exercises of moderate intensity are probably better for the average nonathlete. Once a certain threshold level of intensity is reached, improvement in aerobic capacity will be similar for activities performed at lower intensity–longer duration compared to higher intensity–shorter duration, if the total amount of energy expended, measured as caloric expenditure, is the same.

Now what is this about "maximum heart-rate reserve?" On the average, the maximum heart rate of a given individual is about 220 minus age in years. Thus an average 20-year-old would have a maximum heart rate of 200. Suppose an athletic 20-year-old has a resting pulse rate of 50. Heart-rate reserve would be 150 beats per minute (200 minus 50). To exercise at 60 percent of heart-rate reserve would mean exercising hard enough to push the pulse rate (60 percent times 150 plus 50) to 140 beats per minute. For older persons, this value may be 110 to 120 beats per minute, since the maximum possible heart rate is less. All of the above exercises are capable of producing an adequate pulse rate if pursued intensely enough.

As a cyclist, I'm also interested in any specific effects these exercises have on cycling. Anything that involves mostly leg muscles especially front thigh muscles, will keep legs strong for cycling.

Keeping in mind all of the above considerations, I can refer back to the examples of exercises given by the American College of Sports Medicine:

# Bicycling: Seize any opportunity to cycle, including a winter vacation to southern climes.

# Running: Use running shoes if the roads are clear. If snow covers the roads, use hiking boots. Running uphill is better than running on level ground, because it will strengthen the quadriceps. But don't work too hard or you might get hurt.

**Walking–Hiking:** This doesn't get the heart rate up very high, so you must keep at it for a longer period of time. A long hike with a backpack could be strenuous, though.

**Swimming:** Although swimming doesn't do much for the legs, you could swim at a local indoor pool once in a while.

**Skating:** Speed skating is excellent for cycling muscles, but you may have trouble locating facilities in your area.

**Cross-Country Skiing:** This may be the ideal winter exercise for the cyclist, if there is enough snow. But it requires some investment in equipment. Money can be saved by using wider skis which take cable bindings and by using the hiking boots you may already have.

**Rope-Skipping:** It is a very strenuous exercise; ideal for the traveler as it can be done indoors or outdoors.

**Endurance Games:** I take this to mean handball and the like. These are fine if pursued with great intensity and high heart rate. But such activity may also require a court, partner, and some equipment.

For me, an ideal winter regimen involves a variety of exercises. I take a two-hour lunch every other day, which gives an hour to cycle, run, swim, or work out at a gym. On free weekends I plan some strenuous outdoor activities such as skiing or running, and on my on-call weekends I can still get out and chop wood. If I'm out of town I take along my bicycle or at least a pair of running shoes.

It's been found that even a fairly strenuous weight-lifting program isn't of much value for cardiorespiratory fitness; the periods of exercise are too short and the rest periods too long. Any exercise chosen has to be continued for at least 15 minutes at an adequately high heart rate to maintain aerobic fitness.